IT'S A SIGN!

Seeing Jesus in the Ordinary

Timothy W. Fisher

PublishAmerica
Baltimore

First printing

Unless otherwise noted, Scripture quotations are taken from the New International Version © International Bible Society, 1973, 1978, 1984; used by permission.

At the specific preference of the author, PublishAmerica allowed this work to remain exactly as the author intended, verbatim, without editorial input.

ISBN: 1-4241-5531-2
PUBLISHED BY PUBLISHAMERICA, LLLP
www.publishamerica.com
Baltimore

Printed in the United States of America

~ This book is dedicated to Tammy Smith,
whose faith in this season of adversity is a sign to me ~

Table of Contents

Chapter One: Experiencing Jesus in the Ordinary
9

Chapter Two: Beginning at the End
17

Chapter Three: Water, Wine, and a Wedding
25

Chapter Four: Experiencing the Jesus Who Disturbs Me
39

Chapter Five: An Invalid and an Invasion
55

Chapter Six: Experiencing Jesus Who Fills Me
67

Chapter Seven: I Once Could See but Now I Wonder
81

Chapter Eight: Dead Man Walking
93

Chapter Nine: The Death of Religion
111

Endnotes
125

IT'S A SIGN!

Seeing Jesus in the Ordinary

Chapter One

Experiencing Jesus
in the Ordinary

*In the right light, at the right time,
everything is extraordinary.*
−Aaron Rose

I'm not sure why it is, but as long as I can remember I've enjoyed taking tests. Didn't matter what the subject matter was. Didn't matter if I'd Ace it or end up looking like the Joker. I've always enjoyed taking tests. Right now as I sit to write this chapter at a *Panera* Restaurant I have run into two of my former teachers; one from middle school, the other from high school. Both are now retired. The middle school teacher was my first Home Economics teacher and I remember making a felt football in her class that had my name and future graduation year on it. Nineteen eighty four seemed an eternity away at the time. The high school teacher taught me Physical Science; not one of my stronger subjects, and no felt footballs were made in her class. I wonder if these two teachers know that I really do like taking tests.

One of the tests that I remember from my earliest test taking days had to do with word associations. For example, there may be four words in order that look like this: Apple Banana Cucumber Pear. My job as an elementary aged scholar was to circle the word that didn't belong; the word that didn't quite fit with the rest. The way to get to the answer was to see what three of the items had in common, and which item didn't quite fit with the other three. As little wheels in my mind turned I'd recognize that three of the items were all fruits, and the item that didn't fit was a vegetable. If you're wondering, the word above that doesn't fit is Cucumber.

I have listed some life experiences below. Take a few minutes and see if you can find what they might have in common. Don't worry; it's not a real test for those who may have taken tests in school with dry throats and sweaty palms.

- Celebrating a college graduation at a restaurant.
- Hearing an old song on the radio.
- Thinking about someone all day and then having that person call me.

- Reading two books which confirm something I've been thinking about.
- Sharing the pain of a friend who confided in me of a loved one's homosexual stuggles.
- Struggling with and going through bouts of depression.
- Praying an ancient way of prayer called *Lectio* with a Benedictine monk.
- Sitting through a Twelve Step meeting as an invited guest of a friend who is celebrating sobriety.
- Recognizing that deeper and sometimes darker part of me that I'd rather avoid.
- Running through the rain with my kids to get to our mini-van and then observing the rainbow afterwards.
- Participating in *Career Day* at the local middle school.
- Watching an episode of television's *American Idol.*

More could be written, but these will suffice. In addition to these being ordinary moments of life where names, places and faces could be changed to match most anyone's experiences in life, these were all moments for me in the past several months where I've experienced something of Jesus in the ordinary of life. It may have been a moment where I recognized something of His grace. It may have been a moment of recognizing His Presence; or His love. And yet all these moments happened during times that were downright ordinary.

Notice that some of these times were times of celebration

(celebrating a college graduation, sitting through the Twelve-Step meeting). Other times were definitely not celebratory and were even painful (bouts of depression, sitting with a hurting friend). Some of the moments were what we might refer to as spiritual in nature (praying with a monk, times of inward reflection) whereas some would not be considered spiritual (hearing an old song on the radio, watching *American Idol*). Some of these times were more personally internal (thinking about someone all day, reading coincidental books), while others were experienced in the company of others (running through the rain, participating in Career Day). Yet each one held for me a moment in time; a "freeze frame" if you will, of experiencing something of Jesus in the ordinary.

Ask anyone how he experiences something of God's Presence and his answer may depend on his denominational (or non-denominational) background, religious affiliation, previous experiences, or what he has been taught. For example, I was raised in the Roman Catholic tradition and was a part of this heritage until around the age of 19. To this day I know many wonderful Catholic brothers and sisters in Jesus and I pray regularly with a Catholic monk. A Catholic's response to, "How do you experience Jesus?" might be, "I experience Jesus through the Eucharist, when I partake of the body and blood of Christ," through the sacrament of confession, or perhaps through one of the other sacraments.

Another part of my varied heritage of Christian

spirituality is my experience with the Charismatic movement that swept through the Catholic Church in the 1960's and 1970's. Our local Catholic Church experienced this in the mid to late 1970's and celebrated this new kind of spirituality through a prayer meeting that was held in the basement of the church. I was in my early teens at the time and it was at these Friday night meetings that I learned of the life in the Spirit; the raising of hands in worship; a personal relationship with Jesus; and, of course, speaking in tongues. Ask someone who has experienced this phenomenon how he experiences Jesus and he might answer, "I experience Jesus through praise and worship," "I experience Jesus through the gifts of the Spirit," or "I experience Jesus through the Word."

Another piece of my religious experience has been with the Brethren in Christ Church, of which I have been a part of as the pastor of a local church in Walkersville, MD for nine years. The Brethren in Christ have a rich history of following the practices of Jesus in current culture through loving one's enemies in active peace and non-resistance, living simply, and endeavoring to live out the teachings and example of Jesus in daily life. Ask a member of the Brethren in Christ church how he experiences Jesus and the answers would likely be varied as these expressions of faith can also lead to an experience with Jesus in the ordinary.

Another part of my spiritual life that I was introduced to sometime early in my trek through Christian spirituality is that of having a daily quiet time. A daily quiet time is a period of the day where in the stillness of the early morning hours the Bible is read, prayers are said, more Bible or devotional material read, and then more prayers recited. I remember during one of these times about a decade ago I prayed through the Lord's Prayer for a couple of hours. If you were to ask me on one of these days of "quiet time," I would answer the question of how one experiences Jesus by explaining the discipline of quiet time and the activities that take place during the time set aside for this.

A couple of years ago during the month of August I engaged in a several day personal retreat at a Benedictine monastery in Washington, D.C. The monks there were very hospitable and invited me to share in their daily routine as much or as little as I desired. I found myself drawn to their five times of daily prayer known as *The Divine Office* where the Scriptures, particularly the Psalms, are chanted. Another practice I learned from my time at the monastery that has greatly enriched my spirituality is an ancient method of prayer called *Lectio,* or *Lectio Divina;* named for the Latin words for "divine reading." I was first instructed in this method of "divine reading" by the Abbot of the monastery and have continued this as a practice in my life. In *Lectio* the Scriptures are read, meditated upon in silence, recited in the form of a prayer, and then contemplated. If you were to ask my Benedictine monk brothers how they experience Jesus, they may answer that they experience Christ through *The*

Divine Office, Lectio, their work, or perhaps their shared life together.

This book affirms all of these and the many other ways in which Jesus is experienced in and throughout our world, yet emphasizes through a series of signs contained in the Gospel of John that experience of Jesus which happens in the ordinary of life: the moments during the day; the week days and the weekends; the work days and periods of recreation; the moments enjoyed (or endured) in the company of others, and the moments spent in quiet reflection alone. These simple lessons were first given as a series of talks to a local congregation so that individuals might better discern the presence of Jesus in daily living. In the time since these talks were given the phrase, "It's a sign," has been expressed to me by several individuals of their experience with Jesus in the ordinary.

These moments of experiencing Jesus in the ordinary are what we could refer to as signs today. Some are signs of His Presence with us. Others are signs of His care for us. Some may be signs of His correction to us. Yet all these signs point to a greater reality; an Ultimate Reality, and that is Jesus Himself.

You are probably reading this book because you are interested in spirituality. Most people are. This book is not limited to those who would label themselves "Christian," as the experience of Jesus is not limited to those who currently follow His teachings. I have heard stories of Muslims seeing visions of Jesus, whom they refer to as a prophet, during times of daily prayer which resulted in an experience with Jesus and subsequent faith in Him. I have read the testimony of Hindu missionaries who have encouraged Hindus to pray to no other god for thirty days except Jesus Christ, and of Hindus coming to faith in Christ as a result.

I have been pleasantly surprised to learn that most people are interested in the person of Jesus Christ, even if they do not call themselves a Christian or claim allegiance to any church. This book is written to anyone who has interest in the historical person of Jesus Christ, and will serve as a simple guide to experiencing Him today. It goes without saying that it is not intended to be the "be all" and "end all" of what it means to experience Jesus. Yet it is my hope that an experience with the person of Jesus will be the result, and that He would be experienced by those who seek Him in greater and increasing measures. If you are a part of a local church, I pray that you might experience Jesus in the context of your local church, whether it is liturgical or contemporary; Quaker or Charismatic; historical or a brand-new church plant. And then I pray that this little book might contribute something to you in experiencing Jesus in the ordinary.

Chapter Two

Beginning at the End

The secret of a good sermon is to have a good beginning and a good ending, then having the two as close together as possible.
–George Burns

In the side door of my eleven year old Saturn sedan is a cassette tape that has turned from white to pale-yellow with both use and age. I've listened to this tape dozens of times. It's an abridged version of a book written in the eighties by a leadership and business sage named Stephen Covey entitled, *The Seven Habits of Highly Effective People.* One of the habits Covey speaks about in the tape is called "Begin with the End in Mind." The idea behind this second of seven principles, or habits, is to start with the end goal in mind before you begin the endeavor, whether it is building a home, a marriage, or a business. Every builder knows this principle as no construction company would allow their workers to just show up on the job to build a brand-new building without a set of blueprints tucked under arm. The blueprints are the guide as to what the house should look like in the end. Likewise, beginning with the end in mind is having a blueprint of what you want and can be applied, says Covey, to marriage partnerships, business partnerships, and life in general.

It may surprise some that almost two thousand years before Covey sold fifteen million copies of his book another author wrote a biographical sketch of the life of Christ by beginning with the end in mind. This author is the Apostle John, the disciple best known as "the one that Jesus loved." It may be of further surprise to learn that biblical authors such as John were not head-in-the-clouds celestial men who wrote in trance-like states, but down-to-earth men who actually thought about their material beforehand; arranged it; checked it out with other eyewitnesses and sources, and then wrote to a specific audience with a set purpose in mind as guided by the Holy Spirit.[1] This is what John and other authors did to give us today what we call the Holy Bible; these men began with the end in mind.

In his gospel John doesn't leave it to guess work as to why he picked up the pen (or whatever he may have used) in the first place as he states the purpose of his writing in summary near the end of the gospel.

Jesus did many other miraculous signs in the presence of his disciples, which are not recorded in this book. But these are written that you may believe that Jesus is the Christ, the Son of God, and that by believing you may have life in his name. John 20:30-31

Did you notice what John says here? It's like he's saying Jesus' entire life and ministry was chock-full of miraculous signs as to Who He truly was; that Jesus did so much stuff during His ministry—so many miracles; so many good things to people in need, and that these things were seen first-hand by His disciples as well as others. But then right as he captures our amazement with the magnitude of this historical person named Jesus Christ he goes on to state that not all of the miraculous signs Jesus did were written in his book. At the end of his gospel he again reminds us of the enormity of Jesus' life by stating that all the books in the world could not contain a record of all the awesome things Jesus did.[2]

I get the impression that John wants us to know just how incredible it was to have followed Jesus, and that it would be impossible to write down everything Jesus did that was amazing and beyond belief; everything that could serve as a "miraculous sign." Then John tells us that "*these* are written…" (italics mine). This statement begs the question, "These what?" The context of this passage answers this question as, "these miraculous signs." John says in effect, "Not everything Jesus did is in this book, but this is a book of miraculous signs that is enough to show you who Jesus really is." The reasons given for recording the miraculous signs of Jesus are then given: that we might believe in His name and that in believing we might have life in Him.

When John uses the word "believe" he's not just talking about a distant mental assent like I might say, "I believe it might rain tomorrow," and then go about my day without any further reflection or real life change. Rather, the word "believe" in the Gospel of John refers to the kind of belief that is backed up by throwing one's entire life into the belief. It is more the kind of belief where I might say, "I just heard a weather report issuing a severe warning of high winds and heavy rain in hurricane-like proportions. We are being advised to evacuate the area as soon as possible." With this kind of warning I then back up the belief with my entire life by leaving work early, boarding up the windows to my home, evacuating the area, and seeking refuge in another county or state as did residents of Louisiana and other states during Hurricane Katrina. This second kind of belief, says John, will lead to life in Jesus; a living, breathing, day-in and day-out experience of the Savior that can happen in the ordinary moments of life. It's like he's saying, "Do you really want to know what life is all about? Do you really want to know the Ultimate Reality of living? Pay attention to the signs I've put in this book, throw your entire self into belief, and experience the life of Jesus for yourself." This is the beginning point to understanding what true Christian spirituality is about.

The Gospel of John, therefore, is more than just a biographical sketch on the historical person of Jesus Christ. It is the gospel of signs; miracles that Jesus did that point to the greater reality of Who He is and, like any other sign, are not the ultimate reality in and of themselves, but rather point to that greater and ultimate reality.

When I was in the third grade my family packed up our 16 foot *Nomad* Travel Trailer for what would be my first trip to Florida. I had saved every penny I could get for this big family trip and had over $ 15.00 in hand. As we traveled south on the interstate I remember distinctly seeing great big signs for a place in Dillon, South Carolina called *South of the Border*. Anyone who has traveled Interstate 95 South through the state South Carolina has experienced this as well as it is near impossible to miss the signs. I recently checked the Internet and discovered that there are over 120 billboards spanning a distance of more than 200 miles that announce *South of the Border*.

Despite the many colorful billboards, the ultimate reality of *South of the Border* is not found in the signs, but in the restaurants, gift shops, and experiences that lie ahead in the place called *South of the Border*. I could get out of my car and take pictures of each and every one of those billboards and still miss the ultimate reality of *South of the Border*. What these signs were created to do for me along the way was simply to grab my attention, invoke my sense of curiosity, and make me thirsty for the experience of the reality itself. Apparently the signs served their purpose as we stopped at *South of the Border* and I spent the first dollar or two of my loot.

Similarly, when John writes of signs, his purpose is not for us to get enraptured with the miracle, or the sign itself, but to get our attention, invoke our God-given sense of curiosity, and make us thirsty for the experience of the reality of Jesus Christ. This experience is found in belief; not of the "it might rain" proportions, but in the hurricane kind of belief that is backed up with life action.

The following chapters of this book center on the signs contained in the Gospel of John; signs which all point to the Ultimate Reality of Jesus Himself. It has been my experience that because these signs point to the Ultimate Reality of Jesus, we too, like those of the first century, can experience Jesus in the ordinary of life and have the Ultimate Reality of life itself. So get ready as you read; fasten your seatbelt; pay attention to the signs along the way, and get ready for the ultimate reality of life itself—to believe in and to experience the kind of life that is only found in the person of Jesus Christ.

Experiencing Jesus in the Ordinary

Using the illustration above, is your belief in Jesus like stating that it might rain, or that a hurricane is coming?

Chapter Three

Water, Wine, and a Wedding

I am as vulnerable and fragile as it is possible to be. I am shred-ded to the core. I am at the point where I am stripped bare.
–Rachel Hunter, ex-wife of Rod Stewart

On the third day a wedding took place at Cana in Galilee. Jesus' mother was there, and Jesus and his disciples had also been invited to the wedding. When the wine was gone, Jesus' mother said to him, "They have no more wine." "Dear woman, why do you involve me?" Jesus replied, "My time has not yet come." His mother said to the servants, "Do whatever he tells you." Nearby stood six stone water jars, the kind used by the Jews for ceremonial washing, each holding from twenty to thirty gallons. Jesus said to the servants, "Fill the jars with water"; so they filled them to the brim. Then he told them, "Now draw some out and take it to the master of the banquet." They did so, and the master of the banquet tasted the water that had been turned into wine. He did not realize where it had come from, though the servants who had drawn the water knew. Then he called the bridegroom aside and said, "Everyone brings out the choice wine first and then the cheaper wine after the guests have had too much to drink; but you have saved the best till now." This, the first of his miraculous signs, Jesus performed in Cana of Galilee. He thus revealed his glory, and his disciples put their faith in him. John 2:1-11

Interpreting the Sign

A small boy was asked the meaning of this miracle where Jesus turned water to wine at a wedding celebration. The little guy replied with a grin, "When you have a wedding, be sure to invite Jesus!" While there is truth and much needed application for marriages in the boy's words, this miracle has much more to reveal than that. The Gospel of John is a book of signs, and John helps us to understand this beginning with the very first miraculous sign that Jesus did.

Therefore, this water-to-wine miracle was done not simply to meet an inconvenience during what was otherwise a joyous celebration, or even to make amends for a social disgrace within culture as running out of wine would have been during the week long wedding celebration. Rather, it was the first of Jesus' miraculous signs and it was through this sign that Jesus chose to reveal His glory to His disciples. It was also through this first miracle-sign that Jesus' disciples put their faith in Him. It's as if John's writing to us saying, "Look beyond the water, the wine, and the wedding. Look at the sign and experience Jesus."

When John states that through this sign Jesus revealed His glory he simply means that this sign, or working of Jesus, revealed something of Who He was and is. Therefore, the word "glory" is a revelatory word, and John uses it in his gospel to unveil something about Jesus. It may be observed that the glory of anyone is shown in his work. The glory of an artist is shown in his paintings; his sculptures; his artwork. Look up at the ceiling of the Sistine Chapel and you will see the glory of Michelangelo. The glory of an athlete is seen in his performance on the field; on the track; or on the court. In my library is the August 9, 1976 edition of *Sports Illustrated,* whose cover features the American decathlete Bruce Jenner after he won both the gold medal and world record. Those who watched the '76 Olympics can probably still picture

Jenner's famous 300 yard sprint at the end of the 1,500 meter event to the roaring of the crowd. In both of these cases it's as if what is on the inside is being displayed outwardly for all to see. In a similar way, something of Who Jesus is and was is revealed through this first miraculous sign and the six signs subsequent to this.

There were at least five implications of this first miraculous sign to those who witnessed it in the first century. For those who were willing to look beyond the surface of the miracle and probe a little deeper, the sign would point to the greater and ultimate reality.

First, this water-to-wine miracle was a sign to the people Israel that her long-awaited Messiah had come and that the dawning of the Messianic age was present come at last. The Jewish prophet Isaiah had foretold some centuries before this time that when the Messiah would come, His advent would usher in a time where rich food and the finest of wine would be supplied for all the peoples of the world.[3]

In other words, this sign pointed to Israel's long-awaited-for moment and announced that the culmination of history and Jewish hope had arrived through the person of Jesus. It was like the chapter in God's story that Israel longed for Him to write was being written through Jesus, the Word made flesh, yet the story God was writing didn't look at all like Israel had expected.[4]

I have a friend who is in her mid-seventies who was widowed several years earlier. Just recently she has begun dating a man around her age that she met through an Internet dating service. A few weeks ago I met her new friend for the first time and together they shared their story with me of how they first connected through the Internet dating service; then through e-mails and phone calls, and then finally of their first date where they saw each other face to face for the very first time. I thought of what that kind of experience must be like, where you first get to know someone's characteristics, their dislikes and their likes without ever seeing what they look like in person. Then I thought of what it must be like when you see them for the first time and compare the actual physical looks of the person to the mental picture you had in mind of him/her.

This was somewhat Israel's experience with Jesus as what stood before her in flesh and blood was so unlike the militant hero that so much of Israel had in mind; a leader who would use the weapons of physical force and rebellion against the emperors and rescue Israel from the hands of her Roman oppressors.

Secondly, Jesus would be for Israel "the Life" that would replace the ceremonial rituals that had become full of form and empty of life. I find it no less than fascinating that when Jesus turned water to wine He did so by desecrating some sacred symbols of first century Judaism. It would stand to reason that if wine had run out at the wedding there would have been plenty of empty vessels lying around to replenish the wine from. Yet John is careful to note that Jesus intentionally chose "six stone water jars, the kind used by the Jews for ceremonial washing." Notice also that these stone jars were empty. The sign, therefore, is that Jesus took something that was totally empty and filled it with something new; something that represented life.

I am amazed when I hear some speak as if Jesus came to destroy Judaism when Jesus Himself proclaimed that He came not to destroy, but to fulfill.[5] For the first-century follower of Yahweh (Israel's God), these stone jars represented the religious Judaism of the day which was filled with tradition and ritual yet lacked the power of God. It is also a necessary reminder to us today that, for whatever our stone jar may be—our worship style, our denomination or non-denomination, our doctrine, our local church, our prayer or meditation—that these must be filled with the life of Jesus lest they become like stone jars; religious symbols that are cold and lacking vitality.

Third, Jesus' water-to-wine sign hints to the Messianic vocation where Jesus would become Israel for the benefit of the world. The nation of Israel at this time had become unfaithful to Yahweh and to the mission He had given her for the benefit of the world. Jesus would speak in reference to this by likening Israel to the salt that had lost its savor and the light that had been hidden under the basket.[6]

In ancient Israel salt that had lost its savor was not completely discarded, but stored in the temple for the rainy winter months. When the smooth floors of the temple courts would become slick from rain, this salt was thrown down much like we throw salt on roads and sidewalks today. Therefore, salt that had lost its savor would inevitably be trampled by men. These words of Jesus would prove to have prophetic significance for Israel as the nation would soon be trampled by the Roman army under a general named Titus. The Jews would revolt against Rome in 66 A.D., only to be trampled for 3 ½ years until the fall of Jerusalem in A.D. 70. It was then that the Temple was reduced to ruins.

Note how the prophet Isaiah describes Israel's deplorable condition; a condition that had reached its apex at the time of Jesus.

> See how the faithful city has become a harlot! She once was full of justice; righteousness used to dwell in her—but now murderers! Your silver has become dross, your choice wine is diluted with water. Isaiah 1:21-22

I believe that the imagery of choice wine diluted with water, which is used here to indicate the unfaithfulness of Israel to her God, coupled with Jesus' first miraculous sign of water being turned into choice wine is unmistakably meant to tie in Jesus' vocation as Israel's Messiah for the sake of the world. Where Israel had become unfaithful, He would become Israel yet remain faithful. Where Israel had become unjust and unrighteous, He would become Israel;

the just and righteous One. Where Israel had become a disobedient son; He would become the obedient Son for Israel and the world. Yet this Messianic picture was so unlike what Israel had expected.

Fourth, the comments of the master of the banquet to the bridegroom concerning saving the best wine until last seem to be reminiscent of the fulfillment of Jesus as Israel's final prophet in a long line of prophets which include Isaiah, Jeremiah, Ezekiel, Daniel and the twelve minor prophets whose books comprise the final dozen books of the Old Testament. Jesus would later refer to Himself as the Prophet-Son in what has been named The Parable of the Talents.[7]

Finally, Jesus' water-to-wine miraculous sign hints to His God-given calling as Israel's Deliverer; that in essence a brand new Exodus was happening in Israel's presence with the coming of Jesus, and that a prophet greater than Moses was present within Israel.[8] It may be observed in light of this that Moses' first miraculous sign was the turning of water to blood, which resulted in the death of Israel's enemies, whereas Jesus' first miraculous sign was the turning of water to wine, which He would later use to symbolize His own blood, the blood which would result in reconciliation and life for the enemies of God.[9]

Experiencing the Sign

Jesus' first miraculous sign didn't take place in the Temple, which was the ultimate religious symbol of the first century. Nor did it take place in the religious setting of the synagogue where faithful Jews would gather to learn and discuss the Torah. Instead, Jesus chose to give this first miraculous sign at a wedding celebration in an insignificant little town called Cana of Galilee. There are at least three connections to our experience of Jesus today as the One Who is Life and the Ultimate Reality of Living.

First, Jesus reveals Himself to those who are weak and fragile. Jesus Himself would later say that he came not for those with a spiritual clean bill of health, but those in need of Him as the Great Physician. Jesus chose to perform this first miraculous sign in a place called Cana of Galilee, a place so insignificant that scholars today aren't certain as to the exact location of it.

The word *Cana* means "reed" and the reed is used in the Scriptures as a symbol of something that is weak and fragile; something that is at its breaking point and in desperate need of mending and healing. There is a beautiful promise in Isaiah 42:3 repeated in Matthew's Gospel of the compassion of Jesus, "A bruised reed He will not break, and a smoldering wick He will not snuff out" (Matthew 12:20).

My time of feeling like that bruised reed and smoldering wick came in the fall of 2005 when my then nine-year-old daughter Chloe experienced unexplainable pain and swelling in her knee which in turn led to a diagnosis we were not expecting. Chloe had been experiencing some pain in her leg, which we interpreted as "I don't feel like playing soccer today." No swelling or bruising was noticeable so we made Chloe suit up and sit with the team on the bench although she didn't play in the game.

As we were tucking her into bed a day or so later we noticed that her knee had swelled up to several times its normal size although there had been no trauma done to the knee. We made a doctor's appointment as soon as possible and through a series of blood tests were informed that Chloe had Lyme Disease. I had known of several persons with Lyme Disease and for each person it had been, and was, a long and difficult illness to deal with. As we were trying to process the ramifications of this, further testing also revealed the possibilities of Juvenile Arthritis and/or Lupus.

Several days later, with the initial shock still echoing in my soul, I decided to get away from the house one morning for a time of prayer. As I was driving I was also praying for Chloe's healing as the radio played softly in the background. When I hesitated in speaking I noticed the words to the song which was playing, which had to do with all things being possible when we call on the name of Jesus. I remember turning up that song louder and louder and louder. And then a peace that passes human understanding filled my heart. To me those words were more than a song; they were the sign of

Jesus Christ, Who still takes care of "bruised reed" people who are weak and fragile and turn to Him.

Second, it may be observed that Jesus reveals Himself to obedient risk-takers. In this first miraculous sign Jesus uses the services of some unnamed servants who filled the jars with water and then drew some of it out for the master of the banquet. Remember that John is detailed in his description of these six stone jars as each having the capacity to hold between twenty and thirty gallons. Given the weight of a gallon of water, each jar of water probably weighed between two and three hundred pounds when filled to the brim. Remember also that these were sacred vessels used by the Jews for ceremonial washing as part of their religious culture and heritage. I get the picture that there was no way to quietly fill these jars in a back room and then sneak them back in to the place where the guests were. It would have taken a few men to carry each one and I can just picture these guys grunting and sweating and moving these jars very slowly from the place where they were filled back to the banquet hall.

Jesus then asks these same unnamed servants to give some of the water to the master of the banquet. Three powerful words are used to describe the obedient actions of these risk-takers for Jesus as they would desecrate sacred vessels and follow foolish instructions: *they did so*. These unnamed servants were willing to desecrate sacred symbols for Jesus. Their actions didn't get them fame or fortune and their names are not even mentioned in Scripture. However, it takes little imagination to believe that their experience with Jesus in changing water to wine also changed their lives.

Like these servants of Jesus' first miraculous sign, Jesus continues to reveal Himself to obedient risk-takers; servants who are willing to follow and obey Jesus even when it becomes messy, unpopular, foolish, or against the grain of religious tradition and status quo.

I think of how much kingdom work gets done by unnamed servants of Jesus. I think of unnamed followers of Jesus who are faithful in their witness, some paying the price of persecution with their own blood. I think of the thousands of unnamed and unfamed pastors serving Jesus in small rural communities. I think of unnamed Sunday school teachers who are doing what Jesus has called them to do, sometimes with little thanks or appreciation.

I recently met up with an old friend name Tricia at a funeral who was the very first Sunday School teacher my teenage son Stephen had when he was of pre-school age. As we reminisced she shared with me that she is now teaching in her pre-school Sunday school class the children whose parents she had in the same class some twenty years ago. As we departed company I was caught up in thinking about the steadfastness of her service. Her name and face may never be on the cover of a magazine, but her work will not go unnoticed by Jesus.

Thirdly, Jesus reveals Himself to those who are thirsty for

more of Him. In obedience to Jesus the servants give some of the water-turned-wine to the master of the banquet which causes him to marvel at how the best wine had been saved for last. The Scriptures state that he didn't realize where the wine had come from. In other words, he tasted of the sign but missed the Ultimate Reality of Jesus!

When we are thirsty for more of Jesus, experiences of His grace become opportunities to taste of the Ultimate Reality of life Himself. It may be a moment of His protection that defies explanation. This was the case of a woman I know named Jenny who walked away from an automobile accident after another vehicle flipped on top of her car not once but twice. I spent time after visiting her in the emergency room thinking about how many people walk away from accidents like that every day yet fail to see the hand of God in this and experience Him through it.

Another experience of God's grace may be a moment of provision for a specific need as I have experienced countless times, most recently when friends gave us an unexpected check when they heard we had become the victims of identity theft. Life moments like these, which have a way of happening in the ordinary of life, become signs that point to an experience with Jesus that awaits us.

Experiencing Jesus in the Ordinary

Where do you feel most fragile?

Where do you feel weak and vulnerable? Or scared?

Where do you feel like you've "run out of wine?"

Where in life are you at your breaking point, like that bruised reed?

Where do you feel like the wick of your life is smoldering?

Where might following Jesus be "risky business" for you?

Where might following Jesus be unpopular or uncertain?

Where might following Jesus seem foolish in the eyes of the world?

What signs have you seen recently of Christ's goodness, His power, or protection?

How might greater reflection upon these lead to an experience of Jesus?

Chapter Four

Experiencing the Jesus Who Disturbs Me

An atheist is one who hopes the Lord will do nothing to disturb his disbelief.
–Franklin P. Jones

After the two days he left for Galilee. (Now Jesus himself had pointed out that a prophet has no honor in his own country.) When he arrived in Galilee, the Galileans welcomed him. They had seen all that he had done in Jerusalem at the Passover Feast, for they also had been there. Once more he visited Cana in Galilee, where he had turned the water into wine. And there was a certain royal official whose son lay sick at Capernaum. When this man heard that Jesus had arrived in Galilee from Judea, he went to him and begged him to come and heal his son, who was close to death. "Unless you people see miraculous signs and wonders," Jesus told him, "you will never believe." The royal official said, "Sir, come down before my child dies." Jesus replied, "You may go. Your son will live."

The man took Jesus at his word and departed. While he was still on the way, his servants met him with the news that his boy was living. When he inquired as to the time when his son got better, they said to him, "The fever left him yesterday at the seventh hour."

Then the father realized that this was the exact time at which Jesus had said to him, "Your son will live." So he and all his household believed.

This was the second miraculous sign that Jesus performed, having come from Judea to Galilee. John 4:43-54

Experiencing the Sign

In this sign John once again gives us a "heads up" as to what Jesus is doing by naming this miracle "the second miraculous sign that Jesus performed." This miraculous sign of healing was done, therefore, not only meets the needs of a desperate father whose son happened to be at the point of death, but to give to us the second sign through which we might believe in Jesus and experience the Ultimate Reality of life itself. There are four experiences of Jesus that await us in this sign.

First, it may be observed that Jesus reveals Himself to those who have "ears to hear." The idea of having "ears to hear" was used by Jesus several times during His teaching ministry as somewhat of a prophetic postscript to His teachings and parables.[10] One of the meanings of this phrase indicated that there was something more to be understood by those willing to probe beneath the surface of the teaching or parable. Therefore, the stories of Jesus contained multiple layers of interpretation and application which invited the listener to discover his place in the story. This principle of having ears to hear can be seen in the way John introduces this second miraculous sign as he does so with a degree of irony.

If we were to look at the context of this second miraculous sign, it is preceded in the fourth chapter of John by a discussion between Jesus and a Samaritan woman; a discussion that was nothing less than scandalous for that time period. In speaking to the Samaritan woman Jesus transgresses long held cultural boundaries and discards acceptable social norms. Yet following this dialogue is some of the most successful ministry Jesus experienced in His three and a half year tenure as an itinerant preacher. Notice this warm reception to the good news didn't take place in Jerusalem, but in the despised region of Samaria.

Against this backdrop John tells us that "after two days He left for Galilee." In other words, Jesus is experiencing ministry at its best. Hearts are wide open. The people of Samaria are now proclaiming Him as Savior of the World. The entire town is experiencing faith in Him. Yet he leaves all this behind Him after two days to go to Galilee; the region where He grew up, the region where He would be received on one level and rejected on another.

Note the irony by which John introduces this miracle. He states that Jesus left Samaria, the place of success, to go to Galilee; the region where He grew up. Most of Jesus' formative years took place here in the little town of Nazareth in Galilee. John then reminds us that Jesus Himself had pointed out that a prophet has no honor in his own country; a fact well attested to by Old Testament prophets. Yet the Scriptures then state that the Galileans welcomed Him. It would appear that instead of rejecting Him according to Jesus' own words, they laid out the red carpet in homecoming celebration for one of their very own.

I have read several commentaries on the Gospel of John regarding this passage. Most commentators try to wiggle out of the well-known fact that Jesus was returning to His own country by making Jesus' "own country" somewhere else other than the region of Galilee. Only one commentary writer I found agreed with my conclusion.

I believe John introduces the second sign this way to reveal to us that although Jesus was warmly welcomed by the Galileans, He was welcomed not as a prophet of God proclaiming the Word of the Lord but as a Miracle-Man performing works of wonder. In other words, they welcomed Him not because they had "ears to hear" but because they wanted to be "wowed" by the excitement of the next miracle; the next healing; the next supernatural deed.

Several years ago I attended a Fall Festival to benefit a retirement community in Pennsylvania. Part of the festivities for families included a husband and wife team who had a magic show that included sleight-of-hand and other tricks. Their magic show was held in a tent that could hold about 100 people or more. There were no seats; we just stood there and watched them "do their thing." For the last act the husband put his wife in a small box and said that he would make her disappear. There were no curtains behind them and they performed this trick on solid ground. The back of the tent was about fifteen feet behind them and I and several others had the ability to see behind them fully. When this man said the words and tapped the box it fell apart and his wife had disappeared. I've always enjoyed watching the antics of magicians and to this day I don't know how he did it. I do remember being "wowed" by the mystery of the experience.

When I think of my experience with that husband and his wife with their magic show I confess that I really had no desire to get to know them as people. I didn't care about their dreams; their vision; their hopes and dreams. I wasn't there to hear anything of substance that they might have to say; I simply wanted to be entertained by what I couldn't understand.

My experience with the magic show comes to mind when I read about the Galileans and how they are described; how they didn't want so much to hear the Word of the Lord through Jesus, but simply to be wowed by the experience and mystery of the miraculous signs. John states above that the only reason they wanted to be around Jesus was because "they had seen all He had done in Jerusalem at the Passover feast." John writes of this Passover feast experience in the second chapter of his gospel.

> Now while he was in Jerusalem at the Passover Feast, many people saw the miraculous signs he was doing and believed in his name. But Jesus would not entrust himself to them, for he knew all men. He did not need man's testimony about man, for he knew what was in a man. John 2:23-25

There were many at that Passover Feast who saw the signs and believed in His name, yet Jesus did not entrust Himself to them. Being a witness to what Jesus was doing did not guarantee them an experience with Jesus Himself. Jesus will not entrust Himself to those who follow signs and wonders and are looking for the next religious "high," but entrusts Himself to those who are willing to hear the prophetic word of the Lord that sometimes (dare I say, oftentimes) is disturbing. I think of those disturbing times in my life where I knew Jesus was speaking to me through His Word about character issues and my character, or lack thereof. I think also of the times when His Word didn't bring comfort to me, but came as a challenge or rebuke; the times where I felt miserable at first before receiving His empowerment and grace. It is times like these that the Word of Jesus comes to us with the roar of the Lion from the Tribe of Judah rather than the gentle voice of the Shepherd Who brings comforts. Sometimes we must first be willing to receive His roar before we receive His comfort.

I have a friend named Aidan who was the abbot, or superior, of a monastery named St. Anselm's Abbey in Washington, D.C. Although he is almost twice my age, we have forged a strong friendship and pray together each month at the monastery. After our times of prayer at St. Anselm's we usually sit around for a few minutes and drink strong black coffee while sharing our lives with one another. During one of these times Aidan shared with me some advice that another abbot gave him almost twenty years ago. This man's advice was to read the Gospels and pay attention to the words of Jesus that disturb him. In doing so, said his friend, he will make a fine abbot. This advice was the voice of wisdom speaking from one friend to another and has been beneficial for me as well. Although my friend Aidan wasn't considering the position of abbot at the time, his friend's words would ring true as Aidan would be appointed the abbot of St. Anselm's Abbey a short time later. My friendship with Aidan bears witness that he has not taken words of his friend in vain.

As I read the Scriptures I am sometimes overwhelmed at the grace and goodness of God. I praise God for Scriptures like Isaiah 26:3 which promise me peace when I am in distress. I cling to the promises of God's protection and provision when I travel, or am in need of resources. I bask in the promises for forgiveness that I read in 1 John and other places when I say or do something that is so unlike Christ. I look to the Scriptures which speak of healing when I'm sick and was greatly comforted by them when praying for Chloe and her healing from Lyme Disease. But a more probing question is, "Am I likewise willing to have ears to hear the Word that might disturb me?" "Do I really have ears to hear?" "Am I willing to experience the Jesus Who disturbs me?"

Secondly, Jesus reveals Himself to those who come to Him not only with requests, but a quest for more of Him.[11] While the request of the royal official reminds us that it is scriptural to bring our requests to Jesus and that we can freely approach Him to receive grace, there is perhaps an even higher calling in coming to Jesus. We could call this a quest for more of Him. Such a quest is demonstrated in the backdrop to the healing of the royal official's son in the interaction between Jesus and the Samaritan woman. Though the following is a bit choppy as it omits part of the story dialogue, you will be able to see the progression of this woman's quest for Jesus.

> The Samaritan woman said to him, "You are a Jew and I am a Samaritan woman. How can you ask me for a drink?" (For Jews do not associate with Samaritans). John 4:9

> The woman said to him, "Sir, give me this water so that I won't get thirsty and have to keep coming here to draw water." John 4:15

> "Sir," the woman said, "I can see that you are a prophet. John 4:19

> Then, leaving her water jar, the woman went back to the town and said to the people, "Come, see a man who told me everything I ever did. Could this be the Christ?" John 4:28-29

Notice how the woman's interaction with the Messiah progresses from cultural questions of interaction between

Jews and Samaritans and the propriety of conversation between the sexes to a request for the Living Water that Jesus offered her. This in turn leads to the perception of Jesus as a prophet and then a pondering of Who Jesus really is, and whether or not He could be the Christ. At this point in their dialogue she isn't requesting anything *from* Jesus, but in her quest she is growing and searching and hungering and thirsting *for* more of Jesus and Who He really is. An experience with Jesus await those who come to Him with a similar quest for more of Him.

Thirdly, we can see that Jesus reveals Himself to those who reject the insidious notion that "seeing is believing." What I like about this royal official is that even after Jesus gives a rebuke about needing signs and wonders to believe (Verse 48), the man still pursues Jesus with his request. Rather than being offended, put off, or having his royal sense of importance bruised as a henchman of Herod, he continues to approach the Lord with humility. After a simple word of healing from Jesus, a man he didn't even know, the royal official took Jesus at His word and departed for home.

Most of us have been nurtured in the world of our senses; a world where "seeing is believing." From promises made to us at an early age that ended up being broken; to the claims of the latest and hottest gadget on television commercials; to the reality that "there's no such thing as a free lunch," we have cut our teeth on the concept of "seeing is believing." The royal official was different. He didn't say to Jesus as perhaps I would have, "Oh, no you don't. You're not going anywhere. I'm not going to let you out of my sight until my kid gets better." Instead, he rejected the "seeing is believing" mentality for the faith-filled belief that "believing is seeing."

When I was a youth pastor over a decade ago we played a game that was based on trust. I never did find out the name of the game, but chances are you've heard of it. It's where one student stands behind another student and the student in front crosses his arms and is expected to free fall into the arms of the student behind. Most of the time the student falling instinctively catches himself rather than trust the person behind him to break his fall. This is yet another example of how often we fail to trust in what we can not see. I discovered the key to this game of blind trust is to let go of what can be seen by shutting your eyes to it. It's as if by blinding yourself to one world (that of sight) you are opening yourself to another world (that of faith and trust).

An experience with Jesus Himself awaits those who are willing to drop the demand for proof and take Jesus at His Word. Jesus longs to reveal Himself to those who cling to the hope that "believing is seeing" (i.e. faith) and reject the soulful demands of the flesh that "seeing is believing." Jesus awaits those foolish enough to close their eyes to the world of sight and open them to the world of faith and trust.

Finally, Jesus reveals Himself to those who are willing to explore amazing coincidences. Another thing I like about this royal servant is even though he discovers his boy is living and has made a miraculous turnaround, he still investigates the miracle. Celebrating his son returning from near-death to life isn't enough for this man. It's as if he is digging beneath the surface of the celebration to experience belief in Jesus. I think it would be easy for the guy to forget all about Jesus in one sense. After all, the only thing he wanted was his boy to be healed and having received a party instead of a funeral should have been enough. Yet he inquires as to the circumstances surrounding the healing in order to explore the amazing coincidence of Jesus' words to him and the exact time of his son's healing. His exploration then leads to belief in Jesus.

There is a scene in the movie *Signs* in which Mel Gibson starred where the two brothers, Graham and Merrill Hess, are talking about the ways in which people view the coincidences of life. Some call it luck while others call it a sign. Then Graham slowly asks his brother the pointed question, "What if there are no coincidences?"

Sometime ago I was talking on the phone with a close friend who asked me if I believe in coincidences, or if every supposed coincidence has the fingerprints of God on it. He was coming to the place in his faith that he no longer believed in coincidences. It has been said that coincidences are simply times that God works and chooses to remain anonymous. I think of coincidences more as invitations from God to move beyond what is seen in the forefront and come "back stage" where an experience with Jesus awaits us.

All of us have experienced an amazing coincidence at one time or another. Have you ever had the experience of having someone on your mind for no apparent reason? As you wake up you think about this person. As you drive to the grocery store this person is on your mind. All day long you think about this person and then the phone rings and it is him (or her). I saw one web site that described this phenomenon as a force of energy in the world that brings this about; like the force of my thinking about this person releases energy which in turn causes them to move toward me in making the phone call. I don't believe it.

Perhaps in this kind of experience there is something more that awaits us than the connection with that person. Perhaps there is an experience with Jesus if we are willing to explore the coincidence.

Six years ago my wife and I were looking for a single family home in our community. At that time there were no homes for sale within our price range and every day I searched the Internet at least a half-dozen times to see what was coming available. The experience was so frustrating and the days were counting down until we had to move. Finally, I realized that God was not at work in my striving, but would be at work if I would surrender the situation to Him. This was one of those times where surrender wasn't too hard since the other option had been nothing short of a waste of time. To make a long story short, God provided a home through a homeowner who contacted me "out of the blue" and offered to sell his home to us. We bought that home and still live there six years later with an awareness of how God's hand was at work when we surrendered our wills to Him. I remember making a statement around the time we got our home that to the unbelieving mind the hand of God is coincidence, but to the believing mind it is God's providence. This statement was printed on an outline sheet to be handed out for the sermon the following weekend at church. The outline was finished before the deal on the home was finalized, and it wasn't until afterwards did I realize that the home God provided for us was located on Providence Circle. What an amazing "coincidence!"

Like the royal official who was willing to explore the amazing coincidence of his son's healing, Jesus still reveals Himself to those who are willing to explore the coincidences of life. It has been said that coincidences are those incidences where God chooses to remain anonymous. I believe instead that many coincidences are modern day signs and invitations to experience Jesus in a deeper way; invitations to go back stage from what is happening in the realm of the senses to what is happening in the realm of faith. It is there that an experience with Jesus awaits us.

Experiencing Jesus in the Ordinary

Am I willing to not only "cuddle up" to what I'm comfortable with about Jesus, but to hear the whispers of Jesus that disturb me, correct me, shake me, and bring change to me?

Where am I coming to Jesus by request?
Am I also coming to Jesus by quest?

Where do I need to take Jesus at His Word?
Where do I need to embrace that in Christ "believing is seeing?"

When did I last wonder, "What a coincidence?"
Could this be my invitation to explore the coincidence and experience more of Jesus?

Chapter Five

An Invalid and an Invasion

Do you want to get well?
–Jesus Christ

Some time later, Jesus went up to Jerusalem for a feast of the Jews. Now there is in Jerusalem near the Sheep Gate a pool, which in Aramaic is called Bethesda and which is surrounded by five covered colonnades. Here a great number of disabled people used to lie—the blind, the lame, the paralyzed. One who was there had been an invalid for thirty-eight years. When Jesus saw him lying there and learned that he had been in this condition for a long time, he asked him, "Do you want to get well?"

"Sir," the invalid replied, "I have no one to help me into the pool when the water is stirred. While I am trying to get in, someone else goes down ahead of me."

Then Jesus said to him, "Get up! Pick up your mat and walk." At once the man was cured; he picked up his mat and walked.

The day on which this took place was a Sabbath, and so the Jews said to the man who had been healed, "It is the Sabbath; the law forbids you to carry your mat."

But he replied, "The man who made me well said to me, 'Pick up your mat and walk.'"

So they asked him, "Who is this fellow who told you to pick it up and walk?"

The man who was healed had no idea who it was, for Jesus had slipped away into the crowd that was there.

Later Jesus found him at the temple and said to him, "See, you are well again. Stop sinning or something worse may happen to you." The man went away and told the Jews that it was Jesus who had made him well. John 5:1-15

Experiencing the Sign

In the third sign of John's Gospel an invalid is healed on the Sabbath, which later invokes the wrath of the religious leaders. It has been observed that it wasn't Jesus' *modus operandi* to go around looking for sick people to heal. It wasn't as if Jesus was looking for publicity, fame, and recognition. Yet there seems to be a pattern in Jesus' ministry that the exception to Jesus searching for people to heal was that he sought out people to heal on the Sabbath; a day where all work was forbidden.

A few months ago I had a conversation with a guest of our Saturday evening worship service afterwards in the parking lot of the church. I had just spoken that evening on Jesus healing on the Sabbath. He made the comment to me that he believed Jesus did so much healing on the Sabbath because that would be the one day of the week where the hearts of the people would be most focused on God. It's as if by doing healings on the Sabbath Jesus was helping people connect the dots as to Who He really was and that this would gain Him more and more followers.

While this makes complete sense logically, and would probably be a good game plan for a messiah looking to fatten his fan club, this was not what Jesus did. In fact, He did just the opposite! He healed the man and then slipped through the crowd apparently to avoid recognition (verse 13). At other times after healing Jesus would instruct the person who was healed not to say anything about what He did. Somehow Jesus didn't find the need to employ today's marketing strategies.

In this third sign I see three other signs which serve are sub-signs to the miracle. Like any other sign, these sub-signs are not a means unto themselves, but reveal the Ultimate Reality of Life itself. In these sub-signs Jesus is revealed, not only to first-century followers but to us as well.

The first sub-sign is the complete absence of angels in this miracle compared to the normal means by which people experienced healing at this pool. The New International Version footnotes the fact that an angel of the Lord would come down and stir up the waters.[12] From there it was a race for all of the diseased to be the first in the pool and be healed of his ailment. You get the picture from the text that it was every man and every woman for himself/herself. Whatever it may have looked like for blind and crippled people to elbow their way to the front when the angel stirred the water, I'm sure it wasn't pretty. Whether or not John Himself believed that an angel stirred up the waters which induced healing or whether he is simply stating common Jewish belief of the first century isn't clear. What is clear is that Jesus healed the man outside of the pool rather than inside of it after the waters had been stirred. What is clear is that Jesus healed the man with a spoken word and not the stirring of the waters.

I have stated before that each sign in John's Gospel reveals something about Jesus and in this sub-sign the superiority of Jesus over the angels is seen. Therefore, there is more being revealed through this sign than Jesus' power to heal; it is a revelation that the power of Jesus Christ is greater than that of angels and that His presence is nearer. The writer of Hebrews would repeat this theme in writing, "So he [Jesus] became as much superior to the angels as the name he has inherited is superior to theirs" (1:4). The Apostle Paul also writes of Jesus' superiority to angels as he writes to the church at Colossai, "For by him all things were created: things in heaven and on earth, visible and invisible, whether thrones or powers or rulers or authorities; all things were created by him and for him" (1:16). Apparently this was written to the church as a safeguard against the teachings of those who were infatuated with angels and would lead the church astray.[13]

As I look on the horizon of current North American culture I likewise see a culture that is infatuated with the concept of angels. The decades of the 1980's and 90's which focused largely on the achievement of material things left people bankrupt of satisfaction as people discovered that the best things in life are not things. Stuff was bought and people who bought the stuff later found that the stuff didn't stuff the inner void they had. Some of these spiritually hungry people then recognized that their hunger was of a spiritual nature, and that it must be filled with something spiritual in nature. For many, their spirituality has been directed to the concept of angels. With the advent of postmodernism spirituality has become focused on anything and everything, and for the first time the masses are looking elsewhere other than the Church to meet this spiritual hunger. The topic of angels has been featured on Prime-time talk shows and popular television programs like *Highway to Heaven* and *Touched by an Angel,* not to mention other television programs which have focused on the paranormal and other spiritual phenomenon. I have seen angels portrayed regularly on the covers of magazines. I have seen web sites promoting conferences on the Internet on how to contact and communicate with angels. One subject that grabbed my attention had to do with what color to wear in order to attract a certain kind of angel!

With the hunger for spiritual things and the infatuation with angels of present day, this third miracle-sign of John points to a greater and more ultimate reality than angels. This is not to say that angels do not have their place in the scheme of God's story, but that the angels themselves exist for the greater and Ultimate Reality of Christ. It's as if this first sub-sign screams to North American culture, "Don't be infatuated with angels. Seek the Ultimate Reality of Life— Jesus Himself!" And the Jesus that we are encouraged to seek is not the watered-down, religiously colored Jesus of many people's upbringing, but a living, dynamic Savior to be experienced in the ordinary of life.

The second sub-sign to this miracle is the invasion of the invalid. Notice that it was Jesus who first noticed the man and not vice-versa, and that Jesus gained some knowledge about the man and his condition in learning that he had been an invalid for thirty-eight years. Some see this as a supernatural kind of knowledge concerning the man; a divine revelation, while others believe Jesus simply asked someone nearby and was told. While Jesus' gaining knowledge about the man's condition may or may not be extraordinary, what He does next certainly is. Jesus does something that no one else would do, not by healing the man, but in asking him the question, "Do you want to get well?"

In my pastoral ministry I have visited all kinds of sick people. I have visited people in nursing homes who were living in their last months or last days. I have visited the elderly who have lived long lives and were nearing death, and I have visited the young who found themselves unexpectedly at death's door. One vivid memory is that of a young man in his early twenties fighting for his last breaths as testicular cancer spread to his vital organs and had shut down his liver. I've been in hospital emergency rooms visiting those with minor bicycle accidents, and I've been in an emergency room where the patient coded by going into cardiac arrest. In all these times and situations it never dawned on me to ask the sufferer, "Do you want to get well?" Talk about an invasion of personal space! You simply don't ask this question to people! You simply don't ask this question *unless* you are aware of something they are not; unless you want to reveal something to them that they're completely unaware of, which is exactly what Jesus did.

I think Jesus knew that this man, like all of us, had an incredible ability to adjust and adapt to negative circumstances. I think Jesus knew human nature and that sometimes we adapt to circumstances rather than receive His best for us. As human beings, God has given us an incredible ability to adjust to adverse circumstances. I remember watching a show on television several years ago called *Ripley's Believe it or Not*. This particular show featured an attractive blonde-haired woman who didn't have any arms. If I remember correctly, she was born without arms rather than losing them in an accident. As she was growing up her mother, instead of babying her or pitying her, challenged her to do things that kids with both arms do— like get dressed in the morning. Try it, and you'll see just how difficult this is to do without the use of upper limbs. As they interviewed this young woman, now a mother; on television the camera showed her changing her baby's diaper with her feet. Additional footage showed her driving her adapted car through a drive-thru restaurant where she paid for her food and received it from the window with her feet. What an amazing ability to adapt!

I've also read the testimonies of prisoners of war and how they adapted to the poor conditions of their captivity, which often included malnutrition, disease, and torture. I saw yesterday on the news the story of a mountain climber who was left for dead on Mount Everest and yet survived. Recently I read the classic, *Anne Frank: Diary of a Young Girl*, which chronicles 25 months of hiding out by a young Jewish girl and her family in the annex of her father's Amsterdam business warehouse when Nazi Germany invaded Holland.

It seems to me that much of the ability to adapt could be attributed to what God has placed within the human spirit to survive at all costs. While these examples are some of the extremes, I think also of those who have adapted to various life experiences, sometimes too well. Some time ago I read the story of a former prisoner of war who was so adjusted to prison life that he barred the windows of his apartment and refused to leave it upon being released. While this an extreme example of adapting to negative circumstances, it serves as an illustration of the many who have adapted in the face of all kinds of abuse; simply settling for something that is less than God's best.

When I was in my late teens I visited a home for girls who had been rescued from the streets. Most of these girls had been involved in drug abuse, prostitution, or homelessness. The friend who had invited me shared with me that even though these girls are receiving the warmth of a home environment, some will return to the streets just because that is what they have adapted to for so long.

While God has given the human spirit an incredible capacity to adapt and adjust to adverse circumstances, it takes God's wisdom to discern where it is in life that God has given me the ability to adjust, and where in life I have settled for something less than His best. Behind the question, "Do you want to get well?" is an invitation from Jesus to experience His best and not what I have adapted to and settled for. An experience with Jesus awaits those who are willing to probe the question, "Do you want to get well?"

The final sub-sign of this trio is what I refer to as the sabotage of the Sabbath. Jesus usually didn't seek out people to heal. It just wasn't His way of doing things. Instead, sick people came to him. One time Jesus, after spending significant time the night before healing the diseases of the sick, moves away from the crowd rather than toward them when notified of the crowd's desire to find Him.[14] The notable exceptions to this rule are those times when Jesus healed on the Sabbath. This, too, was not because the Sabbath was more convenient to Jesus' busy schedule or that the people would be more spiritually attuned, but that Jesus deliberately sabotaged the Sabbath as a sign to Who He was, and what He was about.

When we look at the life of this invalid man and the timing of his healing we see that is was not only a Sabbath, but it was also during the time of a Jewish festival (Verse One). This man was smack dab in the middle of a Jewish celebration, yet he didn't have real joy. He was lying on his mat this day as he had done every day, and yet he didn't have real rest. Jesus' miraculous sign, done on both a feast day and a Sabbath, served to upstage the outward joy and rest that these events brought to point to the inner joy and rest that we all need yet sometimes seek in things other than the living Christ. Jesus further sabotages the Sabbath by commanding the former invalid to violate the Sabbath by carrying his mat. He had been physically unable to do this for thirty-eight years and now, upon being healed, did something in obedience to Jesus that was completely forbidden. Jesus' Sabbath sabotage is a sign to indicate that true joy and true rest are not found in the position of the body or the ceasing from work, but in the position of the heart towards Him. Once again Jesus takes that which was most sacred to Israel and reorients it around Himself and what He was doing. It was if He was saying, "I am your Sabbath. I am your Rest. I am your Joy."

For some of us this may be a needed reminder to not trust in outward things, but to trust in Christ. How prone we are to seek that which we can feel or taste or see! Whether we're seeking true joy and rest in outward things like shopping malls, the Internet, entertainment, possessions, position, or our recreational passion, the result will always be the same: a heart that is less than full of the joy and rest that is allusive. Only the Ultimate Reality of life itself, Jesus the true Sabbath for which the Sabbath Day was but a shadow, can give real joy and rest in their fullness.[15]

Experiencing Jesus in the Ordinary

Who in my life is spiritually hungry yet lacks the knowledge of Christ? What alternate spiritual realities do I see people around me seeking? How would Christ use me as a sign to the Ultimate Reality of Jesus Himself?

Where do I need Jesus to make me whole again? Where in mind, soul, body, or memory do I need His healing? What have I adapted to for so long that Jesus says to me, "Do you want to be made well?"

Am I looking to something other than to Christ for joy and rest? Where is my greatest source of temptation to do this? What is Christ whispering to me about this?

Chapter Six

Experiencing Jesus Who Fills Me

Lord, Thou hast made us for Thyself,
and our hearts are restless until they find rest in Thee.
–St. Augustine

Some time after this, Jesus crossed to the far shore of the Sea of Galilee (that is, the Sea of Tiberias), and a great crowd of people followed him because they saw the miraculous signs he had performed on the sick. Then Jesus went up on a mountainside and sat down with his disciples. The Jewish Passover Feast was near.

When Jesus looked up and saw a great crowd coming toward him, he said to Philip, "Where shall we buy bread for these people to eat?" He asked this only to test him, for he already had in mind what he was going to do.

Philip answered him, "Eight months wages would not be enough bread for each one to have a bite!"

Another of his disciples, Andrew, Simon Peter's brother, spoke up, "Here is a boy with five small barley loaves and two small fish, but how far will they go among so many?"

Jesus said, "Have the people sit down." There was plenty of grass in that place, and the men sat down, about five thousand of them. Jesus then took the loaves, gave thanks, and distributed to those who were seated as much as they wanted. He did the same with the fish.

When they had all had enough to eat, he said to his disciples, "Gather the pieces that are left over. Let nothing be wasted." So they gathered them and filled twelve baskets with the pieces of the five barley loaves left over by those who had eaten.

After the people saw the miraculous sign that Jesus did, they began to say, "Surely this is the Prophet who is to come into the world." Jesus, knowing that they intended to come and make him king by force, withdrew again to a mountain by himself. John 5:1-15

Interpreting the Sign

Some time ago I heard a story about a couple of avid basketball fans who took a trip to French Lick, the Indiana hometown of legendary basketball star Larry Bird. In this town there is a street that leads to the high school where the star used to play ball. The street has since been renamed Larry Bird Boulevard (not a bad improvement on its former name of Monon Street). There is a distinctive street sign shaped like a basketball on Larry Bird Boulevard to announce the pride of the folks in French Lick. It turns out that as this couple was having pictures taken of themselves in front of the sign they failed to notice a jogger passing by that apparently was in the periphery of some of their pictures. That jogger was none other than the 6'9" legend himself, Larry Bird. These two tourists were so focused on the sign that they missed the reality even when he was right in front of their faces!

This same phenomenon happened many times during the life of Jesus. Many people got so focused on the signs and wonders that they missed the Ultimate Reality of Jesus Himself. This was the case of many in the multitude that Jesus provided lunch for on the day of Jesus' fourth miraculous sign.

Jesus' bread-in-the-desert miracle was more than simply a free meal for some hungry people or a lesson on the necessity of being prepared. It was a sign that pointed to

Jesus as the One-Who-Fills and had at least three implications for those in the first century who were hungry for more than just barley bread.

First, this bread-in-the-desert provision was a deliberate acting out of an earlier miraculous provision of bread-in-the-desert for the people of Israel by Israel's God, Yahweh. This earlier account of God's miraculous provision of bread was remembered as part of Israel's history.[16] The timing of God's bread-in-the desert provision is also significant as the miracle takes place shortly after the Passover is instituted for Israel in anticipation and preparation for the flight from Egypt and the slavery of Pharaoh.[17] This story was celebrated in symbol and in festival by Israel century after century for the continual remembrance of God's deliverance of Israel from the land of Egypt. For the ancient Israelite this was more than just an historical remembrance for when Israel celebrated the Passover it was a living history; a celebration of God's deliverance in the past and an anticipation of God's great deliverance for Israel in the future.

It's not an accident or coincidence that Jesus likewise does this bread-in-the-desert sign around the time of Passover (Verse 4). John includes this not simply as a point of reference as to the time of year but as a deliberate connection of this sign to the great Exodus and Passover event. Therefore, by providing bread in the desert Jesus reorients the deliverance of Israel around Himself and the work He was doing for Israel and for the world. He is saying essentially that the yet future Exodus (deliverance) and Passover (forgiveness) that Israel longed for find present and ongoing meaning in Him. He would later emphasize the reorientation of Israel's story around Himself in symbol form on the night He was betrayed through the institution of the Lord's Supper by the breaking of bread and the sharing of wine with His disciples.

Secondly, this sign points to Jesus as Lord and Provider of bread, which stands in opposition to the rulers of the kingdoms of this world. If Jesus was truly the provider of bread then it meant that Caesar was not. This may not sound controversial or dangerous in an age where we often sing songs of Jesus as Lord and Provider but a confession of this sort in the first century would have been looked upon as a political statement against Caesar. In the first century it was Caesar who was proclaimed as lord and the provider of bread. It was Caesar who was your god.

Sometimes emperors would go so far as to include pictures of grain on the coins that bore their image to symbolize that it was the emperor who was your provider of bread. A coin called a *Lepton* from the time of Pontius Pilate, the Roman procurator under Tiberius during Jesus' ministry, features three barley ears surrounded by the name Julia, Tiberius' mother, and her title. Herod Agrippa I, who ruled about a decade after the crucifixion of Jesus, also included three sheaves of barley on the coins that bore his image. Not surprising, Jesus' bread in the desert provision that filled the multitude was also multiplied from small loaves of bread made from barley (Verse 6). And with Jesus, in contrast to the Caesars, there were plenty of leftovers. Thirdly, bread-in-the-desert was a sign that Jesus alone can fill the human heart. This sign would lead to Jesus' Bread of Life discourse, where Jesus would offer Himself as the Bread of Life and invite those listening to partake of His flesh and blood. This call of Jesus has echoes of the call of Yahweh recorded by the prophet Isaiah in the fifty-fifth chapter.

Why spend money on what is not bread,
and your labor on what does not satisfy?
Listen, listen to me, and eat what is good,
and your soul will delight in the richest of fare. Verse 2
Give ear and come to me;
hear me, that your soul may live.
I will make an everlasting covenant with you,
my faithful love promised to David. Verse 3
Surely you will summon nations you know not,
and nations that do not know you will hasten to you,
because of the LORD your God,
the Holy One of Israel,
for he has endowed you with splendor. Verse 5
Seek the LORD while he may be found;
call on him while he is near. Verse 6

Therefore, this sign was an invitation to stop the endless search for what cannot satisfy and to eat of Jesus, the Bread of Life by seeking Him and listening to His Words of life.

In the Arabic language the word for "bread" is so significant that it is also the word for "life" and translation is based on the context of the sentence. By giving Himself to Israel and to the world as the Bread of Life, Jesus is saying that He is "The Life of Life," or in other words, the Ultimate Reality of Life itself. It was this life that He was inviting Israel to seek after, and Israel's call to seek the Lord while He may be found was to be obeyed by looking no further than the One Who was speaking to them and had fed them in the desert.

Experiencing the Sign

The bread-in-the-desert sign also invites us to experience Jesus in the ordinary. By focusing on Jesus' interaction with His disciples in the completion of this miracle we can experience Jesus in the following life applications.

First, the experience of Jesus begins with a willingness to be involved; to take a risk. Last year I took my second son, Jason, on a special weekend to Baltimore, MD. The highlight of the weekend was attending an Orioles baseball game at Baltimore's Camden yards, where we sat five rows back from the field near the first base dugout. After the game as we were leaving the ballpark we happened to notice a homeless man with a cup in his hand. He wasn't standing; he was sitting; almost lying down in a prone position as the crowd leaving Eutaw Street passed him by like a river passes by a rock mid-stream. Jason and I stopped, kneeled down and introduced ourselves to this man. He introduced himself in turn. After a few minutes of casual conversation and a contribution to his cup we departed company. From the time I left the homeless man to the time I found my van in the parking garage I was struck with two dominant thoughts. First, that in this brief interaction of a couple of moments I was experiencing a "God moment." It's not as though I could put my finger as to why, but I just had a sense of God's presence and felt close to God. Second, I was struck with the reality that I might have just as easily missed out on this experience. I might have passed him by like most other people that night and as I had done in times before this, and in doing so I would have missed out on the experience of Jesus. For reasons I'm still not sure of I stopped; got involved if only for brief moments; took a small risk and through the experience met with Jesus.

Most often we think of the great sacrifices for God, like my friend Betsy who is going to Africa for six-months to minister to AIDS babies at an orphanage. I applaud her for this and admire her courage and faith to leave the comforts and familiarity of the life she has known for the journey that lies ahead of her. We need more people like her in this regard. But I am also reminded that sometimes our sacrifices to God are in bite-sized chunks of time where we hit the pause button in our busy schedule to peer into the face of another.

Philip is the first disciple of Jesus to get involved in this miracle-sign. It's not as though he volunteers or is the first to raise his hand. Jesus initiates his involvement by asking him where in the world they were going to buy bread for this hungry bunch. Notice that for Jesus this miracle was not a "Me" deal, but a "We deal." He didn't say to Philip, "Now stand back Phil and be amazed. I will now make bread appear out of thin air" like a magician or some charlatan. Instead, He included Philip in the process of the miracle. Could it be that Jesus asks this of Philip just to get him involved? Could it be that Jesus wants to involve me in bringing "bread" to another? In my encounter with the homeless guy in Baltimore the "bread" I gave him was a few minutes of my time, conversation, and a few bucks. But to him it meant the world. I know because he told me so.

Like the many varieties of bread which serve as a staple food in cultures all over the world, the "bread" that Jesus may use us for to provide to another comes in many varieties. It may be our influence and knowledge. Just recently I was the beneficiary of "bread" when my friends Olivia and Heather used their influence and knowledge in some key meetings at my son Stephen's school. I don't know what I would have done without them. Another great source of bread to others is as simple as having a listening ear. We've all had conversations with others where we had the sense that they weren't really listening to us, but simply waiting to say what they wanted to say. It is a rare gift to give or to receive the gift of listening.

The experience of Jesus awaits those who are willing to get involved in Jesus' "We" deal. This requires risk and involvement of resources and time. My experience has been that these moments are never at a convenient time and I wonder if they come when they do simply to remind us of what's most important in life. Yet I also find that when I am willing to pay the price of involvement the experience of Jesus far outweighs the cost of inconvenience.

Another experience with Jesus happens when I realize the gap between my thinking and His. After Jesus asks Philip the question of where bread would be purchased from for the crowd, the Scriptures tell us that Jesus already had in mind what He was going to do. Philip's answer was calculated as He answers Jesus with the hard cold facts. When you compare Philip's answer to what Jesus finally does to meet the need, it's easy to see that there is a gap between the thinking of Philip and that of Jesus.

I wonder if some of the biggest tests in life are parallel to this, where my mind moves in one direction and Jesus has something totally different in mind that He wants to reveal.

My mind is very practical, natural, down-to-earth, and bottom-line whereas the mind of Jesus is sometimes none of the above. There was nothing practical, natural, down-to-earth, and bottom-line about feeding a multitude of five thousand men and their families with little or no resources! And that was exactly what Jesus had in mind.

In view of how there is often a gap in my thinking and that of God, I decided to look in an online Bible commentary for the verses of Scripture where God specifically speaks of His thoughts and how He thinks. It seemed to me that if I could find some information as to how God thinks I might be able to close the gap. I could find only two references.

One of those was in Isaiah where God speaks of His thoughts as being so much higher than ours.[18] The other verse was found in the minor prophet Micah, and that verse essentially said the same thing.[19] Therefore, I concluded that the gap between my thinking and His is bridged when I recognize this and trust the heart of God in my circumstances even when I can't understand or make sense of it all.

A final thought is that experiencing Jesus sometimes begins with what I already have, not with what I need. The second disciple to be involved in the miracle was Andrew, Simon Peter's brother. Andrew bails Philip out by offering what was already present; a little kid's *Lunchable* of five barley loaves and two small fish. When I read this I thought of the contrast between multiplying what was already present and the temptation of the enemy who tempted Jesus to make something out of nothing; to create bread from a stone, which perhaps resembled bread in size and shape.

The principle here is to offer to Jesus what is already in hand. If I am in need of a financial provision, what will I offer to Jesus so that He may multiply it? This is where faith moves from the realm of mental assent to life action. If I'm in a financial crunch it's easier to clutch what little I have close to my chest, much like what this little boy could have done with his lunch. Instead, he gave his lunch to Jesus and experienced the miracle. If I am in need of a relationship provision, what will I offer Jesus to multiply? In what way is calling me to put Him first in the relationship? If I'm trusting God for a better position at work, what can I offer Him in my present position that He may work in it? This is a principle that can be applied in any area of life.

An experience with Jesus awaits those who take their "five barley loaves and two small fish" and offer it to Him. If I clutch these close to myself this is all I will ever have, and I doubt that if the small boy had done this his lunch would have satisfied any of the grown men present. However, if I offer these to Jesus for His multiplication the result will be much like that on this desert day, where the people all received "as much as they wanted."

Experiencing Jesus in the Ordinary

Where is Jesus inviting me to be involved; to take a risk?
What "bread" is Jesus inviting me to bring to another with my involvement?
In what area of life is Jesus calling me to His "We" deal?
Am I willing to risk knowing that the experience of Jesus outweighs inconvenience?

What challenge or problem am I facing that I may need to rethink my thinking?
In what circumstance of I need to close the gap between my thinking and that of Jesus?

What do I already have that I can present to Jesus?
Where do I need to put God first in order to experience His provision and blessing?
What is my "five barley loaves and two small fish?"
How can I offer these to Jesus?

Chapter Seven

I Once Could See
but Now I Wonder

On my income tax 1040 it says 'Check this box if you are blind.' I wanted to put a check mark about three inches away.
—Tom Lehrer, Humorist, singer, and songwriter.

As he went along, he saw a man blind from birth. His disciples asked him, "Rabbi, who sinned, this man or his parents, that he was born blind?"

"Neither this man nor his parents sinned," said Jesus, "but this happened so that the work of God might be displayed in his life. As long as it is day, we must do the work of him who sent me. Night is coming, when no one can work. While I am in the world, I am the light of the world."

Having said this, he spit on the ground, made some mud with the saliva, and put it on the man's eyes. "Go," he told him, "wash in the Pool of Siloam" (this word means Sent). So the man went and washed, and came home seeing.

His neighbors and those who had formerly seen him begging asked, "Isn't this the same man who used to sit and beg?" Some claimed that he was.

Others said, "No, he only looks like him."

But he himself insisted, "I am the man."

"How then were your eyes opened?" they demanded.

He replied, "The man they call Jesus made some mud and put it on my eyes. He told me to go to Siloam and wash. So I went and washed, and then I could see."

"Where is this man?" they asked him.

"I don't know," he said. John 9:1-12

It was during a Memorial Day weekend of camping with friends named David and Kim that I happened to meet the family whose RV was parked in the site next to mine. I was in the middle of pitching three tents when I met this husband and wife couple. They were warm and friendly and had four children similar in age to my four. Not only that, their dog looked similar to my dog, which was the common ground that sparked conversation in the first place. My dog is a Shih-Tzu, and their dog was a Shih-Poo, which means it is a hybrid breed between a Shih-Tzu and a Poodle, not that their dog is better for the environment. During our brief conversation they shared with me that there were as many as forty to fifty of their friends camping with them this weekend. I immediately thought that they must know all these people from church, because, after all, where else would you know that many people? You may know that many people at work, but who wants to go camping with co-workers?

So in my nonchalant manner I asked them how they and their forty plus friends know one another. I wasn't surprised when they said that they knew one another from church. "Oh," said I, "and what church do you belong to?" "We belong," said they, "to the Kingdom Hall of Jehovah's Witnesses." We talked a little longer, and I left wondering if I was going to have a *Watchtower* pamphlet under my windshield wipers the next day, or perhaps a knock at the entrance of my tent. It turned out that they pretty much kept to themselves and to their friends, although we did get to say goodbye on Monday as everyone was packing up to go.

Afterwards I began to think of some of the other contacts I've had with Jehovah's Witnesses; particularly some several hour long meetings in my townhouse home when I was a seminary student wanting to write a paper on their history. I also thought of how I think they're wrong in their spirituality of who Jesus is, and how they must think I'm wrong in my spirituality of who Jesus is, and that we could reason back and forth for hours without either side budging. Then I thought about how one of us (or both!) are blind to the truth about who Jesus is (I still think it's them).

This led to further wondering about how most of us, like the blind man in this fifth sign, are blind to something even though it's probably not physical blindness. There are four "wonderings" in particular that my camping experience with the Jehovah's Witnesses and the reading of this fifth sign have led me to think upon.

Experiencing the Sign

First, I wondered then and I wonder now, what it is that I'm blind to. Although I still think my understanding of Jesus as God incarnate is correct, I wonder what it is in my life that I'm blind to. I wondered what attitudes there may be lurking within that I'm blind to. I wondered what opinions I may be holding dear that blinds me from being open to the opinions of others. I wondered what viewpoints I possess and if what my view points to is really nothing but stubborn pride. I didn't beat myself up over this but it did make for some interesting musings. I do know that we are never so blind than when we think we can see clearly; when we think that we're right and everyone else is wrong, like the way some people are when it comes to politics or how they're raising their children.

Later on in this story Jesus says some pretty sobering words against the religious leaders who thought they had it all right when it came to who Jesus was. He said, "For judgment I have come into this world, so that the blind will see and those who see will become blind" (Verse 39). So the sign meant that there would be those who are blind, like the guy in the story, who would see and then there would be some who could see (like the religious leaders of the day) but through pride, arrogance, and their opinions would become blind as to who Jesus really is. It's kind of interesting to think that the ones who thought they could see were really blind and the blind ones who thought they could not see were not as blind as they thought.

There is an interesting comparison and contrast in this story between what the blind man said about Jesus and what the religious leaders dogmatically asserted about Him. On three occasions in this story the blind guy (now a seeing guy) admits his ignorance and limitations of his knowledge about Jesus, while the Pharisees in arrogance act as though they know everything about Jesus and become their own final authority on the matter.

The Pharisees

Some of the Pharisees said, "This man is not from God, for he does not keep the Sabbath." But others asked, "How can a sinner do such miraculous signs?" So they were divided. Verse 16

The Blind Guy

"Where is this man?" they asked him. "I don't know," he said. Verse 12

A second time they summoned the man who had been blind. "Give glory to God," they said. "We know this man is a sinner." Verse 24

He replied, "Whether or not He is a sinner or not, I don't know. One thing I do know. I was blind but now I see!" Verse 25

Then they hurled insults at him and said, "You are this fellow's disciple! We are disciples of Moses! We know that God spoke to Moses, but as for this fellow, we don't even know where he comes from." Verses 28-29

Jesus heard that they had thrown him out, and when he found him, he said, "Do you believe in the Son of Man?" "Who is he, sir?" the man asked. Tell me so that I may believe in him." Verses 35-36

What a marked difference there is in the Pharisees, who thought they could see with their smug attitudes, and the blind guy who knew he was once blind. This former blind man was beginning to see in two different ways. His brand new eyes were adjusting to the light of the sun as all he had previously known was darkness, and his spiritual eyes were adjusting to the light of the Son as he was growing in His knowledge and experience of Jesus. An experience with Jesus awaits those who are humble enough to admit even the slightest possibility of their blindness and are willing to receive new sight from the Lord.

The second wondering I have these days is I wonder who it is that I'm blind to. Not just *what*, but *who*. In a sense the disciples of Jesus were blind to this man, for whereas Jesus saw the blind man they saw a conversation piece and begin to have a theological discussion about the man. The disciples saw the blind man and began to speak *about* the man rather than speak *to* the man. There is a great scene in the movie, *Patch Adams*, which reminds me of this. In this scene Patch, who is played by Robin Williams, is in a teaching hospital with other interns and is being led around to various patients by one of the head doctors. As they are walking in the hospital they come across a woman lying on a gurney in the hallway. The head doctor then grabs her medical chart and begins to babble on about her diagnosis and her prognosis and probably some other gnosis. Patch then quietly asks the head doctor what her name is. He asks so quietly that the doctor asks him to repeat the question. When he does, the flabbergasted doctor who was just spitting out information about her Diabetes searches the charts and mumbles that her name is Margery. Patch then goes on to greet her by name and treat her as a person rather than an illness.

The disciples were somewhat like that head doctor when they spoke to Jesus about the man rather than speaking to the man, and their questioning centered on rabbinical discussions of the time. There were some Rabbis who taught that if a child was born with a malady it was because of the sins of the parents. Others taught that a child could sin in the womb as a fetus. Still others borrowed from Greek thinking and believed in the preexistence of souls and wondered if a preexistent soul could sin against God before life in the womb. And the conversations went round and round.

The disciples were not the only ones at fault. I wonder how many other people passed this man on a daily basis yet were blind to him. I wonder how many other people saw him on one level and were completely blind to seeing him on a different level. It's as if they saw him but didn't really see him; more like seeing through him as though he were invisible yet at the same time visible. And the same thing happens to people today.

A few months ago my wife, Beth, and I celebrated our 18th wedding anniversary by taking a bus trip to New York City. The trip was sort of a "no agenda" type of day where outside of meeting the bus at 7 PM in front of Macys, we were free to roam about the city. Some people on our bus visited Ground Zero. Others shopped. We attended a Broadway play and then shopped.

As we were nearing the end of our stay I happened to notice a woman bent over in an almost ninety degree angle.

This woman was dependant upon the compassion of others as she held out her Styrofoam cup. I probably stared at her more than my mother taught me to, but I couldn't take my eyes off of how disfigured she was although she probably was less than thirty years old. I noticed how the toes of her shoes were pointing in toward each other. I noticed how gnarled her wrists and hands were as she clasped onto her cup. I noticed how long and how dark her hair was and the tone of her skin, and I guessed her to be from the Middle East. I ended up putting some dollars in her cup out of compassion or maybe as a payment for the way I stared at her. She mumbled something of thanks. When I saw her again several minutes later she was leaning against a brick building eating Burger King French fries presumably purchased with the money from her cup, and she was eating those French fries with the etiquette of a small hungry puppy. I don't say this to be mean; that's just how she looked to me all hunched up against that building.

Manhattan has a population density of over 66,000 people per square mile. As I thought of this woman I wondered how many people each day; each hour; maybe even each minute pass her by with not so much as a second glance. I wondered how many people passed her by and talked about her without ever giving a thought of speaking to her. I wondered how many New Yorkers and how many tourists saw her without really seeing her. Then I wondered who it is that may be in my life that I see with regularity but don't see them the way Jesus sees them, or the way Jesus wants me to see them. I wondered who I don't see but who it is that Jesus takes great interest in.

I also wonder why it is that I am sometimes blind. I use the word "sometimes" because I think that when it comes to this kind of seeing and this kind of blindness most of us are not either/or but rather both/and. Our sometimes blindness to the people around us are like the times when we're blinded by the sun when driving as our eyes catch its glare.

While the disciples were off as to the cause of this man's blindness, they were correct in stating that sin causes blindness; spiritual blindness. We can be blinded by sin, or we can be blinded spiritually by other things. I think of those who have been blinded by guilt, refusing to receive the forgiveness that Jesus has to offer them. I would imagine that the blind man's parents lived under a tremendous load of guilt because of their son's blindness given the rabbinical teachings of the day. I wonder how many times they looked at their infant son; and then their little boy; and then their young man; and then their grown son and wondered if it was because of their sin he couldn't see from birth; that it was all their fault.

Greed is another sin that can blind us when we get so caught up in things that we fail to see that the best things in life aren't things. Selfishness can blind us as well, which is the malady of humankind. Addictions, the real American Idols, blind us to the reality of their bondage among other things.

We can even be blinded by our strengths, as was Samson in the Old Testament. So I wonder sometimes why I am blind; why I can't see Jesus. And in my wondering I take hope and great comfort in the fact that while I sometimes cannot see Him, He sees me.

Finally, I wonder where it is in my blindness that God wants to display His greatness to me. Jesus' answer to His disciples is that it wasn't the parents' sin and it wasn't the man's sin, but that this happened so that the work of God might be displayed in his life. I don't think Jesus was saying that say that God made the man blind just so He could one day get glory as if God needed the attention. I think this is more of Jesus' way of dismissing the question and the fruitlessness of its discussion. It's like he's saying, "Wrong question, fellas. God is about to do a mighty work in this man's life, so don't get caught up in the blame game." Perhaps the areas in our lives that we question so deeply are the same ones that God wants to display His power. Perhaps our greatest area of pain and confusion, where we seem to be so blind to the reason why, is the very place God wants to display His greatness in our lives. Perhaps the greatest comfort is not in knowing the reason why, but in knowing that even when we can't see clearly and when we can't see Jesus, He sees us and displays the work of God to all those willing enough to admit their own blindness. I hope I keep this attitude, so that in my blindness I can experience Jesus, the One Who causes me to see.

Experiencing Jesus in the Ordinary

What are you blind to that keeps you from really seeing? What attitudes? What worldviews? What sin? What strength or weakness?

Who in the world may be the person you see, but don't really see? Who is it that you don't see, but Jesus takes great interest in? Who do you speak about rather than speak to?

Why are you sometimes blind?
Why can't you see Jesus?

Where may God want to display His greatness in you? What area of pain? Confusion? Blindness? Uncertainty? Where can you take comfort that Jesus sees you?

Chapter Eight

Dead Man Walking

The report of my death was an exaggeration.
–Mark Twain

Now a man named Lazarus was sick. He was from Bethany, the village of Mary and her sister Martha. This Mary, whose brother Lazarus now lay sick, was the same one who poured perfume on the Lord and wiped his feet with her hair. So the sisters sent word to Jesus, "Lord, the one you love is sick."

When he heard this, Jesus said, "This sickness will not end in death. No, it is for God's glory so that God's Son may be glorified through it." Jesus loved Martha and her sister and Lazarus.

Yet when he heard that Lazarus was sick, he stayed where he was two more days. John 11:1-6

On his arrival, Jesus found that Lazarus had already been in the tomb for four days. Bethany was less than two miles from Jerusalem, and many Jews had come to Martha and Mary to comfort them in the loss of their brother. When Martha heard that Jesus was coming, she went out to meet him, but Mary stayed at home.

"Lord," Martha said to Jesus, "if you had been here, my brother would not have died. But I know that even now God will give you whatever you ask."

Jesus said to her, "Your brother will rise again."

Martha answered, "I know he will rise again in the resurrection at the last day."

Jesus said to her, "I am the resurrection and the life. He who believes in me will live, even though he dies; and whoever lives and believes in me will never die. Do you believe this?"

"Yes, Lord," she told him, "I believe that you are the Christ, the Son of God, who was to come into the world." John 11:17-27

Jesus wept. John 11:35

Jesus, once more deeply moved, came to the tomb. It was a cave with a stone laid across the entrance. "Take away the stone," he said.

"But, Lord," said Martha, the sister of the dead man, "by this time there is a bad odor, for he has been there four days."

Then Jesus said, "Did I not tell you that if you believed, you would see the glory of God?"

So they took away the stone. Then Jesus looked up and said, "Father, I thank you that you have heard me. I knew that you always hear me, but I said this for the benefit of the people standing here, that they may believe that you sent me."

When he had said this, Jesus called in a loud voice, "Lazarus, come out!" The dead man came out, his hands and feet wrapped with strips of linen, and a cloth around his face.

Jesus said to them, "Take off the grave clothes and let him go."

John 11:38-44

I didn't watch my first episode of *Sesame Street* until I was well past the average viewing age of six. This was because *Sesame Street* came on Channel 20; at that time Cable TV, and we did not have access to Cable where we lived. My grandmother lived "in town" and she had cable. When we visited Grandma, I'd sit with wide-eyed wonder at all the TV Shows I was missing by living in what must have been the boondocks; shows like *Batman* (where my vocabulary was expanded to *Biff!, Pow!, Smak!* and the like), *Tarzan* (where I learned that one man with a vine could outmaneuver a hundred others with spears), and, of course, *Sesame Street* (I already knew my numbers and ABC's but picked up the Spanish word *agua*). Although I was a little older than most viewers (probably around 9 or 10 years old at the time), I enjoyed watching the antics of the *Sesame Street* gang with Grover being my favorite character.

It was several years after my short-lived viewing of Big Bird and company that death came to *Sesame Street* and not in the way it does on soap operas where one character dies and is reincarnated into another character on a different soap opera. The actor's name was Will Lee, and his show name was Mr. Hooper; the owner of Mr. Hooper's store. Early in the show Big Bird would greet him by the wrong last name; something that rhymed with Hooper, like "Mr. Cooper" or "Mr. Scooper."

Mr. Hooper's death left the producers of *Sesame Street* in a dilemma as to how to communicate the concept of death and dying to its listening audience of ten million plus viewers; most of which were under the age of six. After consultation they decided to avoid giving reasons for Mr. Hooper's death such as "Mr. Hooper was sick" because people get sick all the time but do not die. They also avoided telling the children that Mr. Hooper died because he was old as six year olds view their thirty year old parents as being old. Nor did they say that Mr. Hooper went to the hospital and died because people go to the hospital all the time and do not die. In addition it was decided not to bring in religious themes such as "Mr. Hooper died and went to heaven" or "Mr. Hooper's in a better place." What, a place better than Sesame Street?

They did decide, however, to deal with the subject of death head-on by acknowledging the loss of Mr. Hooper, the grief that accompanies the loss of a loved one, and the permanence of death; that Mr. Hooper was gone and would not be coming back to *Sesame Street*. The resulting show, entitled "Farewell, Mr. Hooper," aired on Thanksgiving Day in 1983 so that parents could watch the episode with their children. "Farewell, Mr. Hooper" had such an impact on viewers that it was named one of the top ten most influential moments on daytime TV by the Daytime Emmys.

In one scene Big Bird has homemade pictures for his friends on Sesame Street. After handing out all the pictures except for the last one Big Bird asks where Mr. Hooper is. After being told that Mr. Hooper died, Big Bird responds by telling them he will give Mr. Hooper his picture when he comes back. In a moment of tenderness Bird Bird is then told that Mr. Hooper isn't coming back; that when people die they don't come back.

The sixth sign of John's Gospel adds a P.S. to that

statement—that when people die, they don't come back—or do they? In this death-to-life sign Lazarus, a friend of Jesus, is raised from the dead and serves as a foretaste of Christ's own miraculous death and resurrection. This "dead man walking" story, as miraculous as a miracle can be, contains more than a death-to-life testimony like those who have experienced death and have claimed to see a great white light. This story is a sign as to Who Christ is.

Prior to the miracle Jesus tells His disciples that what would take place with Lazarus would be more than a death-to-life miracle; that it would be a sign. Lazarus' sickness would be for "God's glory so that God's Son may be revealed" (Verse four). The words "glory" and "glorified" are key words in His statement to understanding the "sign" nature of the miracle.

Different pictures and meanings probably come to mind when we think of the words "glory" and "glorified." We may think of the glory of God an extremely bright light or a type of glow surrounding God, much like the painted halos and auras of medieval religious art. Or we may think of the glory of God as being praise to God, as if God being glorified means that God is praised. While God being praised may be true of God being glorified, the word means more than that, especially for John. In this gospel the word means that there is something about to be revealed about God and His Son. This is the language of signs; that Lazarus' sickness would reveal to the Jews witnessing it, and to us of this century, something about Jesus. In this dead-man-walking story there are three portraits of Jesus for us to probe, ponder, and experience.

Experiencing the Sign

The first picture the sign reveals is a picture of the human face of Jesus. This is not the typical pictures of Jesus that I've seen which make Jesus look like a fair-skinned American. This picture of Jesus is the picture of compassion and reveals the Jesus whose face is streaked with tears.

After a significant four day delay in which Lazarus sickness ends in death and burial, Jesus arrives in Bethany and is confronted by the grieving sister of Lazarus named Martha. "If only you had been here..." she laments. It was as if she was saying to Jesus, "Lord, where were you when my brother died?" "Lord, where were you when I needed you most?" Jesus' response to Martha was not defensive. He didn't say something like, "Look here, Martha, do you have any idea how difficult it is being the Messiah? Try it for just a day!" Instead, Jesus' response to Martha, after a brief discussion about the real meaning of resurrection, was one of tenderness and tears.

For some reason I've spent more time this year thinking about the events of 9-11 than any other year except for the last few months of 2001 itself. In April 2006 the movie

United 93 opened in local theatres, and I felt driven to see it. I don't know why. It was like I just had to see it and relive that day. When I did see it, I watched it with my Associate Pastor Richard and told him that we would talk about leadership after the movie. We were going to watch the movie and then reflect upon the heroes aboard the flight and talk about leadership principles. We never did. It just didn't feel right after seeing the movie. Then in June I read the book *Let's Roll,* which tells the story of a young man named Todd Beamer. Todd was one of the heroes aboard Flight 93 who helped plan a counterattack against the terrorists who had taken over the plane. It was this counterattack that caused the plane to crash outside of Shanksville, Pennsylvania, rather than crash into another building, presumably the White House.

If we look back on September 11, 2001, we can all remember where we were, what we were doing, and what we did afterwards when we received the horrific news of the terrorist attacks. I remember abandoning all attempts of studying for my next sermon, leaving my office to get the kids out of school early, and watching television news reports for the rest of the day in the company of friends and family. I remember the impromptu prayer meeting at church that night and a prayer meeting a few days later that included the local churches of our community.

I also remember the following Sunday when I addressed the horror of 9-11 in our local church by seeing it through the words of Martha in the form of a question, "Lord where were you at 8:45 AM?" That was the question that lurked within our hearts, wasn't it? "Lord, where were you when the first plane hit the tower?" "Lord, where were you as hundreds of gallons of fuel exploded and reduced to ashes the lives of innocent people?" "Lord, where were you when people fell to their deaths on that day?"

I have found that the "Lord, where were you" question is also one of the deepest of the human heart. The young woman who is a victim of rape asks, "Lord, where were you?" The teenager who witnesses his parents' bitter divorce asks, "Lord, where were you?" The parent who loses a son or daughter in an automobile accident due to the reckless driving of a drunk cries out in anguish, "Lord, where were You?"

It has been a teaching in the church for centuries that we mustn't question the Holy One. The witnesses of the Scriptures, however, teach us otherwise. A lot of Bible people did in fact question God in the midst of calamity. Job, one of the earliest books written in the Old Testament, is the story of a man who questions God continually after he loses his entire family, possessions, and health. The greatest example in Scripture, however, would be Jesus Himself when He would in agony question God with words so intense that the gospel writers who recorded it switched from writing in the common Greek language of the day to Jesus' native Aramaic tongue. With parched throat and life escaping His human body Jesus cries out, *Eloi, Eloi, lama sabacthani,* "My God, My God, Why have You forsaken me?" (Matthew 27:46; Mark 15:34).

Martha's statement reminds me that it is only human to question God when faced with the unimaginable horrors of life. Jesus' response of a face streaked with tears further reminds me that the One Who heals our pain also *feels* our pain; that in the moment of our greatest hurt; our greatest betrayal; our deepest wound He *was* there and His face was streaked with tears. The tear stained face of Jesus gives human face to a Savior Who understands when we feel forsaken by God because He's been there.

What a contrast there must have been at the gravesite of Lazarus between Jesus and others who were mourning. In ancient Judaism it was customary to have professional mourners present who were paid to lament and wail over the loss of a loved one. This was done to ensure consolation and that the name of the dead would be remembered. It is against the backdrop of paid professional mourners that Jesus' tears fall from His face in deep sorrow at the loss of His friend.

Jesus' tears also remind me that the ability to weep with and for others is one of the noblest characteristics of genuine humanity. I don't like to cry; I never have. I can remember as a little boy wanting never to have anyone see me cry. Although I wasn't taught this directly from anyone else that I can remember, crying was embarrassing; a sign of weakness; something that sissies do. Not crying was a sign of a big boy, or so I thought. When I was in my first year of middle school we watched the movie, *Brian's Song,* in school as a special. The movie is the story of two football players from the Chicago Bears, Brian Piccolo and Gayle Sayers, who forged a friendship despite different skin colors during the racially charged late 1960's. During the storyline Brian Piccolo discovers that he has cancer, and at one point Gayle Sayers weeps unashamedly upon receiving an award in speaking about Brian Piccolo. I remember being touched in my emotions during the movie to the point of tears but I knew I couldn't cry. After all, I was right in the middle of school and there were tough guys who wouldn't approve! Somehow, despite the touching story I didn't shed a single tear. I had succeeded! Or had I failed?

Now I am inclined to think that perhaps I am never more like Jesus than when my face is streaked with tears as I identify with the pain of others; the pain that Christ not only heals, but feels.

A second portrait of Jesus seen in the sign of a dead man walking is that of Jesus, Who is the Resurrection and the Life. In response to Jesus' affirmation that Lazarus would rise again, Martha responds by stating her belief that her brother would indeed rise again on the last day. Like most faithful religious Jews of the first century, Martha believed in a future resurrection of the dead. This was not the ancient

Jewish equivalent of "dying and going to heaven" and was more than just the belief than an individual would be raised to life again. Except for the Sadducees, most Jews believed the resurrection was a time yet future where the righteous would be raised to new life and live in the world to come. This would also be a time where God's enemies would be defeated once for all, true righteousness and justice would prevail and pervade, and God would rule. It would be the long-awaited day when God's kingdom would come; when God's will would be done on earth just as it is in heaven.

Jesus' response to Martha is both shocking and revolutionary as He took that great future hope of resurrection and molded it around Himself and what He was doing. He was actually claiming to be the Resurrection and the Life and that belief in Him was the basis for life that even death itself could not defeat. The early church likewise preached Jesus and the resurrection and the two themes were so united that pagan philosophers misunderstood the Apostle Paul to be teaching about two different gods.[20] This, too, caused a great disturbance among the Jews, for to do so was to attribute Jesus as the linchpin upon which all of history and hope hang; that He was the one that would be the fulfillment of Daniel's prophecy concerning the son of man and the kingdom of God.[21]

Martha viewed the resurrection as an event; Jesus reveals the resurrection to be a Person. Martha viewed resurrection as something to take place at the end of time; Jesus reveals resurrection to her as something to be experienced in the here and now. Another writer of Scripture, the Apostle Paul, picked up on this theme and wrote the following after the resurrection of Jesus on Easter Sunday.

> And if the Spirit of him who raised Jesus from the dead is living in you, he who raised Christ from the dead will also give life to your mortal bodies through his Spirit, who lives in you. Romans 8:11

Like John, Paul views Jesus as the Resurrection and Life for the here and now; that Jesus through His Spirit can and will give empowerment and life to living bodies now, not just dead bodies later on. Resurrection power is available now for areas of life that seem lifeless, and an experience with Jesus awaits those who believe and seek Him for that resurrection life and power.

The third portrait of Jesus that the dead-man-walking sign reveals is the picture of Jesus Who empowers His Church for His work of resurrection. Jesus, the Resurrection and the Life, has come not to make bad people better people, although that does indeed happen, but to make dead people alive and full of His kind of life.

When the corpse of Lazarus received the breath of life through the spoken word of Jesus, he came forth from the tomb still wrapped with his grave clothes on. There were strips of linen and a cloth around his face. In other words, he looked like a mummy! Jesus' instructions to those who were witnesses of this death-to-life event were to take off the grave clothes and let him go.

The sixth sign is a foreshadow of Jesus' own resurrection, and there are similarities between the burial and resurrection of Lazarus and that of Jesus. Both were buried in a tomb. Both had a stone seal on the entrance of the tomb. Both had been dead for several days, which was a confirmation of death in Jewish thought in the first century as many Jews believed that the spirit of the deceased would stay near the body for a period of days and then depart.

There is one marked difference between the resurrection of Lazarus and that of Jesus, however. When Jesus' disciples peered into His tomb early in morning they saw His grave clothes neatly folded and left in the grave; both the head piece and the body linens.[22] When Lazarus was called forth in resurrection he was still bound with the remnants of death and needed the help of others to aid him in the transition from life to further living. Jesus Himself didn't remove those grave clothes but commanded those who had witnessed the dead man walking to do so. What a scandal this must have been to the first century Jewish mindset as to touch anything associated with death was to incur uncleanness. Jesus' lesson here is that when He does the work of resurrection in the lives of people, not in making bad people better dead people alive, He includes the Church in removing the vestiges of death and that we need not fear contamination.

I have to admit, with sincere apology, that for much of my life as a follower of Jesus I have seen the church and myself, as part of the church, approach certain kinds of people with a fear of their grave clothes. I agree with the words of sociologist Tony Campolo and others who have urged the Church to apologize to the homosexual community for the ways we have treated them that have been harsh and unloving. I think it is time for the church to engage in loving and constructive conversation and life-building ministries because this is exactly what Jesus would do. I think it is time for those of us to stop distancing ourselves from those we work with who are far from God; those who drink more alcohol than they should; those who sleep in more wrong beds than they should; those who are living with their boyfriend or girlfriend, or have other lifestyle choices that indicate their proximity to God. It's just what Jesus would do.

If the Church could be likened at all to a cocoon, it is not that we should be isolated and insulated from the world, but that we should be transformed into something that we're not and engage in the transformation process of others as their grave clothes are being removed. I think this was the foundation of Jesus' statement of calling to His disciples in making them "fishers of men."[23]

A few months ago we had to postpone most of our

weekend services and activities due to inclement weather. The crowd was much smaller that morning than usual as most stayed home to shovel snow. During the message that morning in our later worship service I shared with that small crowd a story about Tony Campolo and an experience he had in the middle of the night at a diner in Honolulu. As Tony was having coffee at this diner a bunch of prostitutes came in and sat around him. Overhearing their conversation, he learned that the following day was the birthday of one of the prostitutes and that she had never had a birthday celebrated before. Instead of leaving the diner to get away from these "sinners," Tony decided right then and there to throw a birthday party for this woman of ill repute. As I shared this story with the church, something came over me and I began to weep. I could barely finish the story and the message. That something that came over me was the presence of Jesus, and I'd like to think that some of those tears were tears of repentance.

I remember telling the church that morning that I want so much to be a part of a church like that; a church that throws birthday parties for whores and welcomes those struggling with addictions, whether to alcohol, sex, or substances. I want so much to be a part of that company who help Jesus by unwrapping the grave clothes of those whose lives He's transforming. After the service I felt embarrassed for getting all emotional like that but I wouldn't trade that experience with Jesus for anything.

Jesus likened the process of unwrapping the grave clothes to fishing for men. In my experience with fishing I know that fishing is a messy venture as the hands and sometimes the clothes get worm stuff and fish gunk on them. Sometimes it hurts when the barbed hook sticks the one with skin rather than the one with fin. And it's far from sterile. Yet this is the metaphor Jesus used to describe the process by which He invites us to be involved with Him in the work of life transformation. An experience with Jesus is present for those who engage in this messy and sometimes painful calling. Maybe in the church we could shed our Sunday clothes just for one weekend and dress in what we might wear to go catch fish, just as a reminder that we are not only to celebrate Jesus as the Life through our worship, but to remove the vestiges of death in others through mission and discipleship. Many grave clothes have yet to be unwrapped, and I want to experience Jesus by being a part of what Jesus is doing as the Resurrection and the Life.

Experiencing Jesus in the Ordinary

When do you find yourself saying to Jesus, "If only you had been here…?"

Do you really believe that Jesus not only heals your pain, but He feels your pain?

Where may God be calling you to pray for the gift of tears?

With whom are you currently sharing their pain?

Where are you in need of the Resurrection and the Life?

What areas of your life seem to be lifeless? Without direction or hope?

Where may God be leading you to the point of full surrender?

With whom may God be calling you to get involved in the work of resurrection?

What groups of people to you are unclean or untouchable?

How is Jesus calling you to be a fisher for the lives of people?

Chapter Nine

The Death of Religion

*If there is a God, atheism must seem to Him
as less of an insult than religion.*
–Edmond de Concourt

Then the Jews demanded of him, "What miraculous sign can you show to prove your authority to do all this?"

Jesus answered them, "Destroy this temple, and I will raise it again in three days."

The Jews replied, "It has taken forty-six years to build this temple, and you are going to raise it in three days?" But the temple he has spoken of was his body. After he was raised from the dead, his disciples recalled what he had said. Then they believed the Scripture and the words that Jesus had spoken. John 2:18-22

For some it's about multi-colored eggs, an oversized bunny, and baskets filled with candy. For others it's about new clothes, church services, and a dinner table surrounded by extended family. For others still it's about a cross, a crucifixion, and an empty tomb. For most, it's a combination of all of the above.

No matter how you slice it, Easter is a big event that is celebrated in various ways all over the world. I've read that up to 12% of atheists and agnostics are willing to attend an Easter worship service if invited by a friend. So what is Easter really about? Or more importantly, how would Jesus answer the question as to what the events of Easter are about? I think the answers to that question that Jesus gives here may be surprising to some. What if I were to tell you that for Jesus the events of Easter were about the death of religion; the destruction of the temple (or perhaps better said, two temples); the fulfillment of Israel's long awaited hope, and that a chief reason for Jesus' death had to do with His dialogue here with the Jews about the temple?

Interpreting the Sign

For Jesus the events of Easter weekend would be about the rebuilding of a temple and John notes after the resurrection had taken place that the temple Jesus was referring to was His physical body. It is important to remember that it wasn't until after the fact of His death and resurrection did even His closest friends understand He was talking about His physical body. This cryptic saying of temple destruction would then take on a dual meaning as Jesus would later speak about the destruction of the physical temple of stone.[24]

It is difficult for those who have grown up with a western view of Jesus to grasp the subversive and outrageous implications of Jesus' words against the temple. The temple was the focal symbol of first century Judaism, and throughout his ministry tenure Jesus acted in ways that subverted the temple by offering freely what one would normally receive through temple ritual. In this light Jesus' offers of forgiveness are all the more shocking as He usurped the authority of the temple and granted what only God could give through the temple.[25] Forgiveness was something you received through the temple. Forgiveness was something that was granted by God alone. The temple was the physical location of the Presence of God and it was through the temple you received forgiveness of sins. The audacity of Jesus in the eyes of the first century leaders was that He acted as though God were present in Him and that one could receive forgiveness of sins through the authority of His spoken word instead of temple ritual.

Jesus, although referring to the temple of His body in the dialogue above, would later speak about the destruction of the physical temple in Jerusalem. His words of judgment against the temple would literally be fulfilled as the Roman General Titus would march upon Jerusalem, lay siege to the city, and destroy the temple in A.D. 70. Therefore, through Jesus' words as Israel's last prophet we can see that while the temple of His physical body was resurrected in three days, the temple of stones through which God's Presence dwelt and forgiveness was offered was destroyed within a generation of His death. That temple has yet to be rebuilt to this day. A few days ago I viewed a live web cam of the Western Wall, also known as the Wailing Wall, which is the only remaining part of the temple today. Even today many Jews view this site as the most holy place in the world as it is the remnant of the temple. The Western Wall serves as a two-thousand year old monument to the fulfillment of Jesus' words.

Jesus' words about the resurrection of His physical body as the temple coupled with prophetic words of destruction for the physical temple undoubtedly lead us to the conclusion that Jesus believed that the events of Good Friday and Resurrection morning served to replace the physical temple with the temple of His body. That is to say that what one would normally go to the temple for is now found in Jesus.

As part of the worship ritual that took place in the temple the worshipper would be surrounded by temple furnishings such as the Bread of the Presence, the Golden Lamp stand, and the Altar of Incense. Through Jesus' temple replacement, this type of worship would come to an end and in its place would be worship not based on physical location, but worship that is in spirit and in truth; directed to God through the resurrected, living temple of Jesus Christ.[26] When the temple would be replaced with the physical body of Jesus, forgiveness of sins would no longer be attained through the offerings of bulls, rams, and goats, but through the once-for-all sacrifice of Jesus, and in coming to Him as both the high priest and sacrifice.[27] God's Presence, once dwelling within the physical walls of stone, would be manifested fully in the temple of Jesus' body as that destroyed body would be raised to life in three days.

Jesus was put to death partly because of His words against the temple as recorded in the second chapter of John's Gospel. This is abundantly clear from eyewitness accounts of Jesus' trial and sentencing and both Matthew and Mark record testimony about Jesus' words against the temple as being confirmed in the mouth of two witnesses.[28] Jesus was seen as one speaking against the temple through words of destruction and by offering freely what could only be attained through the temple, and for this He was charged with blasphemy and ordered to die.

The natural implication to Jesus' anti-temple movement was that religion as the way to God would come to an end. Israel had long anticipated the day spoken of by the prophet Jeremiah; a day when captivity would finally come to an end and Messiah would rule; a day when a new covenant would be revealed by God; a day when God would write His precepts upon the heart rather than tablets of stone; a day when religion would be replaced with relationship. The day had come to Israel at last but didn't look at all like Israel had anticipated.

Experiencing the Sign

Jesus didn't come to establish a new religion. Jesus didn't come to add the religion of Christianity to the rest, and much of what has been done in the name of Christ has been so unlike Him. Jesus came to put an end to religion; to reveal a brand new way of relationship to God and with God. In the Bible this is called a covenant, or a testament, and the Bible is made up of the Old and New Testaments.

Some of the implications of the death of religion can be found in the writings of the prophet Jeremiah, who anticipated this long awaited time as a day when God would put His law in the minds of people and write it on their hearts rather than on tablets of stone.[29] Therefore, obedience to

God is accomplished and lived out through a dynamic union with Christ. For the first-century religious Jews, obedience was demonstrated in part by what you did at the temple. The problem with this was not in the temple ritual, for this was prescribed by God, but that one could go through temple ritual outwardly and still have a heart that is far from God.[30] That's the problem with religion, or perhaps better said, that's the problem with human nature.

I also thought about my own life and the stuff in my life that needs to be worked on. This led me to ask myself whether my obedience to God is expressed through white-knuckled devotion fueled by human strength or through a dynamic union with Jesus. It seems to me that after being a follower of Jesus for most of my life I still find myself drifting back to the futility of religious ways by trying harder, praying more, reading more; what I call "do-more" theology, rather than being strengthened by the Spirit of Jesus. Jesus described this dynamic union with Him as being led by the Spirit. At another time Jesus likened the influence of the Spirit to the wind.[31] So I figure that trying to please God and obey Him through my own weaknesses is like trying to fly a kite or sail a boat without any wind. On the other hand, a dynamic union with Jesus is like a boat driven with full sails, or a kite carried high by the wind, both of which submit to the power of the wind.

Another implication of Jesus' work in putting an end to religion has to do with my identity as a person. For first-century religious Jews the temple played an important part in their identity as people as there were parts of the temple that Gentiles could not access. Therefore, the temple served to separate Jew from Gentile, and to heighten the sense of identity for the Jewish people. When Jesus replaced the temple with the temple of His physical body this separation came to an end. The Apostle Paul, once from the strictest religious sect of the Jews, would later write, "There is neither Jew nor Greek, slave nor free, male nor female, for you are all one in Christ Jesus."[32] This is not to say that the Jewish people do not have a unique place in the ongoing story of God and it was from the Jews that the Messiah came as Savior to the world.[33]

I think it is worthwhile to ask the question as to what or whom we derive our identity from as a person. I asked myself recently whether my identity is through dynamic union with Jesus, or something else. I think that it comes naturally for most of us to derive our identity from something else other than Jesus, and it starts at a young age. We may find our identity in our abilities. We may find our identity in our relationships. We may find our identity in our work. We may find our identity in our socio-economical status. We may find our identity in our recreational passion.

The problem with finding identity in anything other than a dynamic union with Jesus is that all of these other things can come and go in a moment's notice. Some of my favorite television commercials are for *Nationwide Insurance* and end with the tag line, "life comes at you fast." A star athlete falls down the stairs and busts up his leg. A woman is being transported by the most handsome Fabio in a gondolier down a canal in Venice and suddenly he turns into an old man. A man pushing his son on a swing is suddenly knocked down by the swing as his son has grown into a burly young man. Life comes at you fast, and if our identity is in our abilities, our youthful looks, or in relationships we are building our identity on shifting sand. Therefore I think it is worthwhile to take inventory from time to time to see what it is that gives me identity. God said to Jeremiah, "I will be their God, and they will be my people" (31:33b), and this is what gives me an identity that is built on solid ground.

I think the greatest hunger of the human heart is to know God and the temple was germane to knowing God in the first century. The temple was the place where God's presence dwelt, yet Jesus acted in ways as though the unique presence of God was with Him. He spoke of intimacy with God the Father in ways that were so scandalous to the Jews that they tried to stone Him for it.[34] When Jesus replaced the physical temple in Jerusalem with the temple of His body, He became the means by which we know God. Jeremiah anticipated this day as a day when all would know God, from the least to the greatest[35]

Not long ago I read a book by Tom Rainer entitled *The Unexpected Journey*, which chronicles the life-stories of a dozen people who turned from religious beliefs of varied sorts to a dynamic union with Jesus. Their stories reminded me of the many ways people try to get to know God by trying harder, being driven by the guilt of their religion, and following man-made institutions with religious trappings. Jesus' temple-destruction sign is a fresh reminder to me that God put an end to religion and replaced it with His Son.

Finally, when Jesus replaced the temple with His body He became the place where forgiveness is received. For the first-century follower of God the temple was the place where forgiveness was received as sacrifices were offered on the altar for sin. Therefore, Jesus' offers of forgiveness to those he encountered were anti-temple and signs of the day when forgiveness would be received not by going to the temple but by coming to Jesus. Jeremiah saw glimpses of this day centuries prior to Jesus' death and resurrection and wrote, "'For I will forgive their wickedness and will remember their sins no more'" Jeremiah 31:34b.

A few years ago I learned a simple way to differentiate the person of Jesus Christ from religion. All of religion can be summed up in the word "do" and revolve around what one must do to know God, be forgiven by God, and experience God. The spirituality of Jesus, on the other hand, can be summed up in the word "done" and rests on what Jesus has done for me rather than what I must do for Him. All of the miraculous signs that Jesus did that have been explored in this short book point to this astonishing truth, so that we might know Him and have a life that is full of His life.

If you're brand-new to this experience of Jesus you may want to take a few moments of uninterrupted time to express your desire to get to know Him. Ask Him for forgiveness for the wrong things you've said and done. Tell him of your desire to be a follower of His by expressing a willingness to live under His leadership. This simple kind of prayer is one that many others have prayed before you, and has served as a pathway to Jesus.

After you've prayed this prayer you will want to look for a local church to belong to. Don't get caught up in the denomination or non-denominational name on the door (i.e. religion), but look for a setting where you can learn what it means to follow Jesus as expressed in the Bible. If religion seems to overshadow Jesus there, don't worry and don't just forget the whole idea of church as some have. One time while eating in a restaurant I was served broken glass in my ice water. That experience didn't keep me from eating in restaurants. I simply stopped going where I was served broken glass, and looked for safer restaurants to frequent! So just keep looking until you find a church where you will grow in a dynamic relationship with Jesus and others.

While you're on this journey of experiencing Jesus you will also want to read your Bible; not because it's the religious thing to do, but because the Bible reveals the story; the big picture of God, and instructs us on how to follow Jesus. While the Bible must be seen through the culture of the time written, its principles are applicable regardless of culture. As you read, express your thoughts to God (i.e. prayer) and your desire to live like Jesus. Some people through the centuries have benefited by writing their thoughts out in journaling. A good place to begin would be with the historical accounts of Jesus in this book and honest reflection on the questions following the chapters.

It would probably be unfair to end this book without a picture of what an experience with Jesus will do for you. Earlier this season I was watching the television hit-show, *American Idol*, with my family. This was the last show of the season, and we were all on the edge of our seats to see who would be the next American Idol as only Taylor Hicks and Katharine McPhee remained. As part of this special end-of-season finale, various contestants from the past were brought on as guests of the show; some of which didn't make it past the first round when they auditioned.

One of the former contestants was a look-alike of former American Idol Clay Aiken. He dressed like Clay Aiken; styled his hair like Clay Aiken; was similar in build to Clay Aiken, and sang the same music as Clay Aiken. When given the opportunity to sing on this season finale, this young Clay Aiken look-alike didn't hesitate. As he was singing, simply doing his best to sound like Clay Aiken, the real Clay Aiken walked onto the stage and the two of them finished the song together. I couldn't help but notice that when Clay came beside him, the look-alike sang a whole lot better! It was as if he was created to sing in duet with Clay Aiken.

As I watched this transformation take place before my eyes, I experienced Jesus. In seeing that young man endeavoring to be just like Clay Aiken I saw myself, not because I want to be like Clay Aiken, but because I want to be like this person named Jesus Christ. I really want to be a follower of Jesus Christ and Christian spirituality yet I am often aware of how far I am from that picture of perfect humanity. What is both humbling and hopeful is that when I am aware of how far this wannabe is from Jesus, it is those times that Jesus walks onto the stage of my life and begins to sing the song that I'm so desperately trying to sing. And when all is said and done the song is worth singing because we did it together. I am then reminded that I was created to sing in duet and not solo.

The journey for some may just be beginning as you are a newbie at following Jesus and practicing Christian spirituality. Whether you're at the start or nearing the end of this life-duet, experiences with Jesus await you; experiences to mold you and shape you to be the person you were created to be and to live life the way you were created to live it. Just be sure to keep your eyes open for the signs along the way.

> Jesus provided far more God-revealing signs than are written down in this book. These are written down so you will believe that Jesus is the Messiah, the Son of God, and in the act of believing, have real and eternal life in the way he personally revealed it. John 20:31, *The Message*

Experiencing Jesus in the Ordinary

Does your obedience to God come from gritted teeth and white knuckles or through dynamic union with Jesus?

If your obedience to God were likened to a sailboat or a kite, is the wind of the Spirit present?

From what or whom do you derive your identity? Is this something that can be gone in a moment's notice or something much deeper?

Are you growing in dynamic union with Jesus; not merely an outer knowledge but something much deeper and inward?

Is my heart clean and my conscience clear through Jesus? Do I know that I can be forgiven through Jesus?

Do I really believe? Do I have the assurance of real and eternal life? What is my next step to experiencing Jesus in increasing measures?

Endnotes

[1] Compare to 2 Timothy 3:16a, "All Scripture is God-breathed..." The biblical concept of this is known as inspiration and refers to the means by which the Scriptures were given to us by God through men. I have heard it said that "God breathed into man what man breathed out [on the pages of Scripture]." To exercise the metaphor a bit more, when I inhale I take into my physical body something that is separate from myself of which I am dependent upon, and when I exhale I breathe out something similar yet different as oxygen and carbon dioxide is exchanged between the air and the blood in my lungs. When God breathed into man what was then breathed out on the pages of Scripture, He did so in such a way as to use the unique personalities, experiences, gifts, and styles of each biblical writer to give a unified whole. As with any metaphor, this metaphor is not perfect and can be stretched beyond the breaking point.

[2] "Jesus did many other things as well. If every one of them were written down, I suppose that even the whole world would not have room for the books that would be written." John 21:25

[3] On this mountain the LORD Almighty will prepare
a feast of rich food for all peoples,
a banquet of aged wine—
the best of meats and the finest of wines. Isaiah 25:6

[4] I am thankful for the lectures and writings of N.T. Wright, Bishop of Durham, which have shaped my thinking about Jesus in his original Jewish context of the first century. His works are highly recommended by this author.

[5] "Do not think that I have come to abolish the Law or the Prophets; I have not come to abolish them but to fulfill them" Matthew 5:17. Jesus' words of fulfilling the Law here were a common rabbinical way of saying that He would correctly interpret the Law in word and in action.

[6] "You are the salt of the earth. But if the salt loses its saltiness, how can it be made salty again? It is no longer good for anything, except to be thrown out and trampled by men.

"You are the light of the world. A city on a hill cannot be hidden. Neither do people light a lamp and put it under a bowl. Instead they put it on its stand, and it gives light to everyone in the house. In the same way, let your light shine before men, that they may see your good deeds and praise your Father in heaven. Matthew 5:13-16

[7] See Mark 12:1-12.

[8] Compare to the words of Moses, "The Lord your God will raise up for you a prophet like me from among your own brothers. You must listen to him." Deuteronomy 18:15.

[9] "But God demonstrates his own love for us in this: While we were still sinners, Christ died for us.

Since we have now been justified by his blood, how much more shall we be saved from God's wrath through him! For if, when we were God's enemies, we were reconciled to him through the death of his Son, how much more, having been reconciled, shall we be saved through his life!" Romans 5:8-10

[10] See Matthew 11:15; 13:9; 13:43, Mark 4:9; 4:23, Luke 8:8; 14:35.

[11] I owe this distinction of quest/request to Ben Witherington.

[12] Some less important manuscripts "paralyzed—and they waited for the moving of the waters. 4 From time to time an angel of the Lord would come down and stir up the waters.

The first one into the pool after each such disturbance would be cured of whatever disease he had."

[13]1 "Do not let anyone who delights in false humility and the worship of angels disqualify you for the prize. Such a person goes into great detail about what he has seen, and his unspiritual mind puffs him up with idle notions. He has lost connection with the Head, from whom the whole body, supported and held together by its ligaments and sinews, grows as God causes it to grow." Colossians 2:18-19

2 Two authors who have been helpful to me in understanding postmodernism have been Brian McLaren and Alan Roxburgh.

[14] "Very early in the morning, while it was still dark, Jesus got up, left the house and went off to a solitary place, where he prayed. Simon and his companions went to look for him, and when they found him, they exclaimed: "Everyone is looking for you!"

Jesus replied, 'Let us go somewhere else—to the nearby villages—so I can preach there also. That is why I have come.'" Mark 1:36-38

[15] "Therefore, do not let anyone judge you by what you eat or drink, or with regard to a religious festival, a New Moon celebration or a Sabbath day. These are a shadow of the

things that were to come; the reality, however, is found in Christ. Colossians 2:16-17

This is not to say that those in Christ cannot choose to worship on Saturday, simply that we are not to be bound to do so. I applaud congregations that meet on Saturday and other days of the week as part of their strategic mission.

[16] See Exodus 16:1-36.

[17] See Exodus 12:1-51.

[18] "'For my thoughts are not your thoughts, neither are your ways my ways,' declares the Lord.

"'As the heavens are higher than the earth, so are my ways higher than your ways and my thoughts than your thoughts.'" Isaiah 55:8-9

[19] "But they do not know the thoughts of the Lord; they do not understand his plan, he who gathers them like sheaves to the threshing floor. Micah 4:12

[20] "A group of Epicurean and Stoic philosophers began to dispute with him. Some of them asked, 'What is this babbler trying to say?' Others remarked, 'He seems to be advocating foreign gods.' They said this because Paul was preaching the good news about Jesus and the resurrection." Acts 17:18

[21] "In my vision at night I looked, and there before me was one like a son of man, coming with the clouds of heaven. He approached the Ancient of Days and was led into his presence. He was given authority, glory and sovereign power; all peoples, nations and men of every language worshiped him. His dominion is an everlasting dominion that will not pass away, and his kingdom is one that will never be destroyed." Daniel 7:13-14

[22] "Then Simon Peter, who was behind him, arrived and went into the tomb. He saw the strips of linen lying there, as well as the burial cloth that had been around Jesus' head. The cloth was folded up by itself, separate from the linen." John 20:6-7

[23] "'Come, follow me,' Jesus said, 'and I will make you fishers of men.'" Matthew 4:19I first heard the idea of Jesus making his disciples into something they currently were not in a sermon by Andy Stanley.

[24] See Matthew 23:36-38, 24:1-14; Mark 13; Luke 13:34-35, 19:41-44, 21:5-9; which speak prophetically of the destruction of the temple which took place in A.D. 70.

[25] For example, the healing of the paralytic in Mark 2, which took place in a home.

[26] "Jesus declared, 'Believe me, woman, a time is coming when you will worship the Father neither on this mountain nor in Jerusalem. You Samaritans worship what You do not know; we worship what we know, for salvation is from the Jews. Yet a time is coming and has now come when the true worshipers will worship the Father in spirit and truth, for they are the kind of worshipers the Father seeks. God is spirit, and his worshipers must worship in spirit and in truth.'" John 4:21-24

[27] "Day after day every priest stands and performs his religious duties; again and again he offers the same sacrifices, which can never take away sins. But when this priest had offered for all time one sacrifice for sins, he sat down at the right hand of God. Hebrews 10:11-12

[28] See Matthew 26:61 and Mark 14:58.

[29] "This is the covenant I will make with the house of Israel after that time," declares the LORD. "I will put my law in their minds and write it on their hearts. I will be their God, and they will be my people. Jeremiah 31:33

[30] See Isaiah 1:11-20 and Malachi 1:6-14, where the rituals intended to bring the worshiper close to God had become empty of true worship.

[31] "'The wind blows wherever it pleases. You hear its sound, but cannot tell where it comes from or where it is going. So it is with everyone born of the Spirit.'" John 3:8

[32] Galatians 3:28.

[33] Jesus refers to this in his conversation with the Samaritan woman in John 4:22.

[34] See John 5:18; 10:22-33

[35] "'No longer will a man teach his neighbor, or a man his brother, saying, 'Know the Lord,' because they will all know me, from the least of them to the greatest declares the Lord.'" Jeremiah 31:34a

Printed in the United States
68889LVS00002BA/1-30